Szczepan T. Praskiewicz, OCD

Saint Raphael Kalinowski: An Introduction to His Life and Spirituality

D1366601

CA
B
K
(Ph S)

About the Author

Szczepan T. Praskiewicz, OCD, was born in Chmielnik, Poland, in 1958. He attended the Carmelite Minor Seminary in Wadowice, founded by Raphael Kalinowski, and made his religious profession as a Discalced Carmelite in 1978. Ordained in 1983, he earned a diploma in Mariology and in 1988 completed his doctorate in theological anthropology at the Teresianum in Rome. From 1983 to 1990 he served as Prefect of the Order's International College in Rome. He assisted the OCD Postulator General in the final phase of the canonization process for Raphael Kalinowski, and has published numerous studies on the Saint, including a Kalinowski bibliography and his own Italian translation of Raphael Kalinowski's Memoirs. He now serves as secretary of the missions for the Order at the Discalced Carmelite Generalate in Rome, Italy.

Szczepan T. Praskiewicz, OCD

Saint Raphael Kalinowski: An Introduction to His Life and Spirituality

Translated by Thomas Coonan,
Michael Griffin, OCD, and Lawrence Sullivan, OCD

ICS Publications
Institute of Carmelite Studies
Washington, D.C.
1998

Parts I and II are a translation of
"Raffaele Kalinowski: Tappe Fondamentali di una Vita ed Elementi di Spiritualità,"
an offprint from *Rivista di Vita Spirituale* (Rome, 1990).
Part III contains additional texts from Kalinowski's writings
supplied by the author of this article for the English edition.

Translation copyright
©Washington Province of Discalced Carmelites, Inc. 1998

ICS Publications
2131 Lincoln Road NE
Washington, DC 20002-1199

Typeset and produced in the U.S.A.

Library of Congress Cataloging-in-Publication Data

Praskiewicz, Szczepan T.
  [Raffaele Kalinowski. English]
  Saint Raphael Kalinowski: an introduction to his life and spirituality /
Szczepan T. Praskiewicz: translated by Thomas Coonan, Michael Griffin,
and Lawrence Sullivan.
      p. cm.
  Translation of: Raffaele Kalinowski.
  "Selections from his [Kalinowski's] writings" : p.
  Includes bibliographical references
  ISBN: 0-935216-53-7
      1. Kalinowski, Rafał, Saint. 1835-1907. 2. Discalced Carmelites—
Biography. 3. Christian saints—Poland—Biography.
I. Kalinowski, Rafał, 1835–1907. Selections. English. II. Title.
BX4700.K24P7313 1998
282'.092—dc20   94-29713
  [B]   CIP

TABLE OF CONTENTS

Editor's Preface

This publication has an unusually complicated history, and many people have helped along the way. The author, Szczepan Praskiewicz, OCD, originally published parts I and II as "Raffaele Kalinowski: tappe fondamentali di una vita," and "Raffaele Kalinowski: elementi di spiritualità," in *Rivista di Vita Spirituale* (1990): 214-237, 338-357. These were later combined as an offprint, *Raffaele Kalinowski: Tappe Fondamentali di una Vita ed Elementi di Spiritualità* (Rome: Rivista di Vita Spirituale, 1990).

For the canonization of Raphael Kalinowski in 1991, because of the scarcity of material in English on the new saint, John Sullivan, OCD, asked Thomas Coonan to translate part II for the members of the Washington Province of Discalced Carmelites. Then ICS Publications took up the project and arranged for Michael Griffin, OCD, to translate part I. Subsequently, with the permission of Benignus J. Wanat, OCD, Provincial of the Province of Krakow, Fr. Szczepan kindly agreed to provide pictures, as well as additional texts translated from Polish into Italian for a third part containing selections from St. Raphael's works; these were then translated into English by Lawrence Sullivan, OCD. Finally, Jude Langsam, OCDS, helped in the difficult task of editing (and occasionally adapting) the various sections for mutual consistency and a more idiomatic English style.

We are grateful to all of those mentioned here, and to many others without whom this booklet would not have been possible. May their generous contributions bear fruit in a greater knowledge and love of Raphael Kalinowski.

Steven Payne, OCD

Saint Raphael Kalinowski: An Introduction to His Life and Spirituality

By Szczepan T. Praskiewicz, OCD

I. Fundamental Stages of His Life

For the canonization of Saint Raphael Kalinowski, a figure of great distinction and importance on the Eastern European scene, it seems fitting to recall some fundamental events of his life, a life filled with trials and challenges. We also want to outline the principal characteristics of his spirituality. The purpose of this study is to honor the first Discalced Carmelite friar to be canonized after Saint John of the Cross (in 1991, during the fourth centenary of the Mystical Doctor's death), and to offer a spiritual biography and summary of the spirituality of our new saint.

1. Poland at the Time of His Birth

To understand Kalinowski's life and his heroism, one must know the historical context in which he lived, the social and religious situation of his country. When Joseph Kalinowski (his secular name) was born in Vilna on September 1, 1835, "Poland" had not been on the European map for more than 40 years (since 1795). The Polish-Lithuanian territory, which had been one republic from the time of the dynasty of Jaghello (1385), was brutally divided during the second half of the eighteenth century by three foreign powers: Russia, Prussia, and Austria. The Polish and Lithuanian peoples never agreed to this arrangement, nor did they ever accept this kind of injustice. They showed their patriotic love and unconquerable desire for liberty in continual insurrections against the occupying forces. The Polish General, Henry Dabrowski, backed by Napoleon Bonaparte, organized Polish legions in Italy for the liberation of his homeland. "As long as we live, Poland is not dead," sang these legions in Italy, along with the Poles annexed to the Russian, Prussian, and Austro-Hungarian empires of the "belle-èpoque."

This chant became (and remains to this day) the Polish national anthem. But neither the insurrections (Kalinowski was part of one) nor the legionnaires, nor any political efforts (such as the 1815 Congress of Vienna) succeeded in restoring freedom to the Polish and Lithuanian peoples; each insurrection was followed by years of terror and waves of deportations to Siberia.

This was the fate of Joseph Kalinowski and his brothers. Our Polish national hero, a former Minister of War against Russia, died at Wadowice in Galicia in 1907, clothed in his Carmelite habit. He did not live to see the hour of his country's freedom. Eleven years later, at the end of World War I, came the rebirth of a state and a people who for 123 years had no official existence. In this nation, now free and autonomous, and in the very city of Wadowice, only thirteen years after Kalinowski's death, Karol Wojtyla was born, who would become John Paul II, the pope who beatified and canonized Father Raphael.

2. His Youth

Joseph Kalinowski's childhood and youth were marked above all by the education he received in a good family and at the Nobiliary Institute. The second child of Andrew Kalinowski and Josephine Polonska, he lost his mother when he was only two months old. His father later married his first wife's sister, and had three other children: two sons and a daughter. Unfortunately, Joseph's second mother died when he was scarcely nine years old. His father then married for the third time, and from that marriage four children were born. So Joseph had five brothers and three sisters; his father had nine children to educate. Joseph's third mother was a woman of exceptional gifts of mind and heart. With remarkable tenderness she knew how to love all of Andrew Kalinowski's nine children. These parents succeeded in converting their home, even amid its sorrows and joys, into a center of happiness, building their children's happiness on the foundation of a solid Christian education and patriotic ideals. Joseph, recalling his childhood in his *Memoirs*,[1] stresses both of these aspects[2] of his home life. In fact, his entire life confirms this. The whole ideal of his existence is delineated in these two components: to be a Christian[3] and to be a Pole.[4] The same fundamental values were instilled in Joseph at the Nobiliary Institute at Vilna, where he went to school when he was nine years old, and where his own father was a professor of mathematics. "The Institute," Kalinowski himself relates, "was a private [residential] school and only on Sundays were parents or family members allowed to bring their sons home. Discipline for boarding students was in fact very strict. Except for the Director..., the entire administration of the Institute was in the hands of Polish professors, who conducted themselves with us in an exemplary way. The most esteemed of all the professors was Father Mokrezcki, a Dominican priest, one of the [few] religious still able to remain at Vilna. But our joy at having him as our professor was short-lived. Because of a patriotic sermon he preached for the feast of Saint Hyacinth, he was sent to Siberia."[5]

At the outset, we must emphasize that Kalinowski wrote his *Memoirs* only at the end of his life and, as some have pointed out *sub specie aeternitatis* [from the perspective of eternity], seeking to trace the work of grace in his own *historia salutis* [salvation history]. Despite this, having ever on his shoulders the weight of a harsh life, he considered it opportune to recall in his *Memoirs* some episodes of his youth that clearly demonstrate how his Polish patriotism solidified at the Institute. He even recounts how they threw pillows at a non-Polish professor, imposed by the Russians, who later became one of their spies.[6] But he immediately adds that "these were some 'capers' of youth, with its typical instinct for independence and its defense..., the right of the children of a country they considered to be their own."[7]

His education at the Institute ended in 1850. His brilliant success in his studies led Joseph and his father to consider his going on for higher studies, but this was not easy to accomplish.

3. Soldier by Necessity, Engineer by Choice

During his studies at the Nobiliary Institute, Joseph's special inclination and talents for mathematics and geometry became evident, gifts he had inherited from his father. He wanted to pursue higher studies in this field, but like every other Polish or Lithuanian student he was confronted with a dilemma: either go abroad to study, or enroll in a Russian university. Higher studies, in fact, were not permitted in Lithuania or Poland; one of the first edicts of the Czar closed every Polish and Lithuanian university. Andrew Kalinowski, after seriously considering the matter, proposed that his two older sons enroll in the recently created Higher Institute of Agronomy at Hory-Horki. "My brother immediately agreed with the idea; I, instead, accepted the project very reluctantly, and then mostly because I was aware of the displeasure it would have caused my father to see his first two sons separated."[8]

In fact Joseph did not like the study of agronomy. His marked inclination toward mathematics and the related sciences urged him to go elsewhere for an education and eventually led him to the school of Military Engineering in St. Petersburg. He would have preferred the Engineering School of Roads and Bridges, but enrollment there was already full.

Studies at the Military Academy constitute the saddest period of Kalinowski's life, years marked by a crisis of faith and searching for the meaning of life. His faith, formed at home but now lacking the protection of that environment, began to crumble. Religious indifference was deeply rooted and fashionable in intellectual circles of the Russian capital of that time, and greatly influenced the young student, who was uprooted from his country's cultural and religious environment.

In a letter to his brother Victor from that period, Kalinowski confessed, "I am inclined toward the vanities of this world and am seeking in them a medicine for myself, but I do not find interior peace this way." In the same letter he describes his general state of soul as "a moral malaise."[9] In his *Memoirs* many years later he wrote, "I abandoned religious practices, but from time to time a craving for these things awakened in my soul. But I was not faithful to that interior voice."[10]

He was constantly searching. "I am seeking the spirit but I find matter," he confessed to his older brother.[11] Elsewhere he said that he was drawn to read some religious books, especially the *Confessions* of Saint Augustine, and attended Lenten conferences preached in French by the noted Father Souaillard, O.P.[12] He even made an attempt to go to confession: "Passing by the church of Saint Stanislaus (at St. Petersburg) for the first time, the idea came to me to make a visit for a while. I knelt down near the confessional (I remember it as if it were this very day), but unfortunately there was no priest in it, nor was there a soul in the church. I then began to weep. Profound homesickness invaded my entire being."[13]

The sad period of his studies at the Military Academy ended in 1857. Joseph was awarded the rank of lieutenant and named professor of mathematics at the Academy. But he did not want to stay in that environment that had caused him so many interior crises. He began to want to pursue road and bridge engineering as his vocation, so he accepted an offer to work on building the Kursk-Konotop railroad. Taking his final leave of the imperial capital, he went to Kursk. Only then, as he traversed the swamps and muddy fields of these regions of the Ukraine and Russia for his work, and reflected in solitude, did he discover interior peace. In a letter, he describes his state of mind at the time. "In this solitude I succeeded in forming interior peace within myself, and I confess to you sincerely that this continual work with myself and on myself, far removed from people, produced a great change for the good. I could fully acknowledge the value of familiar religious ideas, and, finally, I turned toward them."[14]

This is the initial stage of the process of his conversion. A few years before his death, looking back on his life, he told us more about this trip to Kursk: "I drew great profit from it, not because of the work itself, for which I was not very proficient, but because of a devotional book that very fortunately fell into my hands. It belonged to a Polish assistant; he had received it from his mother when he was leaving home. Reading this book immensely influenced my soul and it especially reawakened in me feelings of confidence in the intercession of the Most Holy Madonna." [15]

Unfortunately, construction of the railroad was suspended for an indeterminate time (probably due to lack of funds). Kalinowski then left the Railroad Company and was transferred, at his own request (because he did not want to settle in St. Petersburg), to the Command of Engineers near the fortress at Brest-Litovsk. He arrived there in November 1860.

In one sense it seemed that all was going well in his life. During his stay at Brest he was promoted to the rank of captain of the General Staff. But in another sense Kalinowski's days at Brest were very sad, because he was becoming more and more convinced that a military career was not for him. What factors caused this sadness? At Brest, Joseph took note of the sorry plight of Catholics [in communion with Rome], persecuted by czarist powers that often succeeded in involving even the Orthodox Russian Church. He learned that it was precisely at Brest that a union of the Ruthenian Church with Rome had been ratified in 1586, a union of whose destruction he was an eyewitness. In his heart he always had a very vivid desire for the union of the churches. In Brest he also saw the sad plight of youth, especially the poor who could not even study because the czarist government had closed the Polish schools. Joseph then took it upon himself to found a little Sunday school in which he himself became a teacher.

At Brest, finally, Kalinowski became convinced that his place was not in the armed forces of the Czar. He began to think of resigning his rank and commissions and seeking other employment. He was apparently influenced in this matter by witnessing (during his 1861 vacation) a patriotic demonstration against Russian domination at Warsaw, in connection with the funeral of the Polish Prince, Adam Czartoryski. His definitive request for discharge was accelerated by the outbreak of the January (1863) Insurrection.

Kalinowski himself confesses that he "was no longer capable of wearing the Russian uniform while his heart was sick with the knowledge that the blood of his countrymen was being shed."[16]

4. Insurrection against the Czarist Government and Exile in Siberia

Joseph Kalinowski knew better than anyone else the strength of the Czarist army; and he also knew that if an insurrection broke out it would fail. "It was all too clear to his mind's eye what would happen in a struggle of unarmed people against the power of the Russian government, which could command enormous armies."[17] He was convinced that Poland "needed sweat rather than shedding of blood; for already too much blood has been spilled."[18] Conscious of all this, he continually asked himself: "Can I remain passive when so many people have sacrificed everything for this cause, undoubtedly a national cause?"[19] He finally decided to join the insurrectionists, even agreeing to become War Minister for the region of Vilna. At the beginning of June 1863 he found himself at Warsaw with the heads of the National Council of the insurrection. By the time he returned to Vilna, the insurrection had been brutally repressed. Unimaginable terror reigned in the city, introduced by Michael Muraviev, governor general of the Czar, the man who had the Bishop of Vilna, Adam Krasinski, arrested and sent into exile. In just one month Muraviev signed 18 death sentences. He also converted monasteries into prisons, and sent entire villages into exile.[20] In such a context it was not easy to lead the insurgents. Kalinowski concerned himself with only one thing: to save as many lives as possible, and to avoid making conditions any worse for his countrymen. This was his only role in the January Insurrection. He learned that human beings attain their fulfillment by serving others. Inspired by this principle, even though he was not a member of the conspiracy that had planned the insurrection (which he always considered a mistake) he nonetheless joined it with only one intention: to save the insurgents. "Trying to the keep others from committing error, taking no part in committing the great mistake [of the insurrection, since there was no hope of success] and still, afterwards, generously accepting his association with the sad consequences of the error, bearing with the others the penalty for the mistake by not accusing anyone: This was Kalinowski's role in the insurrection." [21]

After being spied on by the Russians for some time, Kalinowski was arrested on the night of March 24–25, 1864, and taken to a nearby Dominican monastery that had been transformed into a prison for the insurgents. He was the last of the leaders of the rebellion still at large. But his was a very serious crime: An ex-captain of the Czar's army, he had become Minister of War against the Czar. Hence the sentence passed by the Military Tribunal on June 2 was the most serious possible: capital punishment. Innumerable pressures from his family and friends, not to mention the great esteem in which he was held by nearly everyone, persuaded the Russians and even Muraviev himself to avoid the risk that he might come to be viewed as a martyr of the people; his death sentence was commuted to ten years of forced labor in Siberia. [22]

On June 29, 1864, began the long terrible march that Kalinowski describes in these words: "On the very feast of the solemnity of the Holy Apostles Peter and Paul, near midday, the long file that we composed snaked its way through the streets of Vilna toward the train station. An enormous crowd lined the streets and Cossacks on horses kept back anyone who tried to come close to us; many people were watching from their windows. It looked like a funeral cortege. But from the beginning of the insurrection how many such convoys had preceded us! Among us were people of every age and every condition.... We took our places in the train cars, where they piled one person on top of another.... When the train departed, people moving along the heights that dominated the railway threw flowers on it as they do on graves of the dead at cemeteries." [23]

When Kalinowski went to Siberia he took a copy of the Gospels, *The Imitation of Christ,* and his crucifix.

It would be difficult to recount here all the details of his trip to Siberia, many of which can be learned from his letters. It's enough to know that this trip lasted almost ten months. Their destination was the salt mines of Usole near Lake Bajkal; they arrived there on April 15, 1865. A few companions in misfortune died along the way, especially after reaching the city of Perm and in the succeeding months. "The city of Perm," Joseph relates, "was a place where they assembled the condemned, and from there they were dispersed throughout eastern Russia. Near the same city of Perm and finally in the Far East, in the immense plains beneath and beyond the Urals, vast and boundless cemeteries were made for tens of thousands of victims who had been taken from the heart of their mother country. There they are buried forever!"[24]

During that trip—or during forced labor in the salt mines of Usole—Kalinowski became a great altruist; in fact, some saw him as an angel of God sent to console the wretched.[25] He knew not only how to bear his own sufferings and discomforts heroically, but also how to share with others the little bit he had. When his meager resources were exhausted, he wrote to his family in Vilna, with apologies: "I write to you sincerely that the misery here is great; it is always easier to find money in the homeland than in Siberia. It is unthinkable for me to remain indifferent to this kind of misery."[26]

During the insurrection and his condemnation to exile he began to cultivate a profound interior life, nourished by frequent participation in the sacraments and personal prayer. Of course, during his exile access to the sacraments was not easy. However, when he was able to receive the Eucharist for the first time after his departure from Vilna, he could not restrain his joy and immediately wrote to his family.[27] Later, during his stay in Usole, when there was no possibility at all of approaching the sacraments, personal prayer sustained his spirit: "Outside of prayer I have nothing to offer to my God. I can't fast, I have hardly any alms to give, I'm unable to work. The only thing remaining for me is to pray and to suffer. But never before have I ever had such great treasures and I desire nothing more."[28]

And it was in Siberia that his vocation to the religious life and the priesthood matured and crystalized; he had been thinking about this even before his arrest.[29] During the summer of 1868, when his amnesty allowed Kalinowski to move from Usole to Irkutsk, he met the parish priest there, Father Szwernicki, who was in exile, and became his valued co-worker, especially in instructing the children of deported families. In his friendship with Father Szwernicki, Joseph deepened his religious culture and studied the history of the church as well as theology, explaining, "If one day it will please the

Lord to call me to the clerical state, I'll have at least some preparation."[30]

Unfortunately, it was not easy to pursue his religious vocation
at that time. Nor was it any easier, after his final liberation from exile
on February 2, 1874, for Joseph to find any novitiate open. All religious monasteries in Poland were suppressed by the occupiers, and
no religious order could admit novices. For Kalinowski there remained only one possibility: migrating to the West.

5. On the Road to the West

Joseph Kalinowski returned from Siberian exile with a reputation as a man of profound faith and upright moral conduct, and a
good educator of the young.[31] This is how his companions in misfortune remembered him, and introduced him on his return from
Siberia. Thus he received many offers to undertake the education
of sons of some noted Polish figures. In fact, while Joseph was still
in exile, Prince Eugene Lubomirski tried through the Russians to
obtain his freedom, because he wanted Joseph in his own house.
Kalinowski, however, preferred another offer from Prince Ladislaus
Czartoryski, who was then residing in Paris. He agreed to assume the
office of tutor for Czartoryski's son, Augustus. And he decided this,
apparently, for one very definite purpose: outside his homeland it
would be easier to enter a religious order. Joseph chose this course
of action against the wishes of his own family, who would have preferred to see him remain closer after ten years of exile. He could
have remained in Poland, but then he would have "cut himself off
from his principal goal of remaining faithful to a decision he had
already taken. But he was determined to persevere in it, and if that
could not be accomplished in his homeland, then it was necessary
to do it in a foreign land."[32]

The meeting with Augustus was fixed for September 9, 1874,
at Cracow. Returning to the old Polish capital, Joseph visited the national shrine of Czestochowa, where he found "an enormous crowd
that filled all the courtyards of the convent and church, and it was
very difficult for him to get to the altar of the Madonna,[33] to offer
homage to our great Advocate."[34] His encounter with the royal city

of Cracow was significant. As Joseph himself related, Cracow made him remember Vilna. He remained in the city for a whole week, visiting the most important and significant monuments of his homeland, such as the Cathedral of Wawel with its tomb of Saint Stanislaus, the patron of Poland; the church of Saint John Kety; the merchants' square with the "Sukiennice," etc.[35]

Joseph and his pupil, Prince Augustus ("Gucio"), travelled for some days to Sieniava (the Czartoryski property in the region of Przemysl), and then to Paris by train, via Vienna and Strasbourg. On October 27, 1874, they arrived at the Czartoryski residence, the "Hôtel Lambert," on the Isle St. Louis. This began a new and relatively brief, but no less important, chapter in the life of Joseph Kalinowski, who was by now forty years old. This period was characterized exteriorly by a continuous pilgrimage from one health resort to another, because Augustus became seriously ill, manifesting all the signs of tuberculosis.[36] On the other hand, this time also led Kalinowski to the Carmelite monastery. Although continually at the side of his pupil and concerned about the boy's material and spiritual needs, he was cultivating a profound interior life. He not only received the Eucharist daily,[37] but even dedicated himself to meditation and reading the great masters of Christian spirituality. Letters written from this period of his life contain quotations from Saints Augustine, Teresa of Jesus, John of the Cross, Catherine of Siena and other authors.[38] At the same time he was also reading books of history and literature, and contemporary spiritual authors, to his pupil. Among these he mentions *The Spiritual Letters of Father Alexander Jelowicki (1804–1877)*, a Resurrectionist Father, celebrated preacher, and religious writer from the Polish diaspora of the nineteenth century. Kalinowski knew him personally[39] and even wrote him a letter[40] that was important in the development of his vocation. Having decided to follow the road of the evangelical counsels, Joseph still had some doubt about which order he should enter. He asked Father Alexander: "What sources should I use to study church doctrine? How should I proceed in this matter? What spiritual practices should I undertake?"[41] We do not know what Father Jelowicki wrote back, but we can suppose that, besides the advice Joseph had requested, he also offered an invitation to enter the Resurrectionists.[42] Some months later Kalinowski wrote to his family: "I have been invited to enter the order of which Father Alexander is a member, but despite the great love of God that fills this order, I haven't been able to discover in myself a vocation to it, or perhaps I haven't known how to cultivate it within me."[43]

How did Joseph come to know Carmel? In his *Memoirs* he tells us that early in his exile he happened upon a book written by Piotr Skarga, *The Lives of the Saints*, "that opened up many horizons for me. There I discovered a note on the Order of the Virgin Mary of Mount Carmel and its rapid diffusion in the West. It occurred to me that precisely this Order should be able to bring the schismatics back to the Church of Rome. Guided in a marvelous way by Providence, I entered this Order ten years later."[44]

Kalinowski was truly guided in a marvelous way. He had wanted to go to the West to find a way to become a friar, which is why he chose to work in the Czartoryski home in Paris. He surely did not know that one of his pupil's aunts, the Princess Mary of Grocholski Czartoryska, was a Discalced Carmelite nun living in the Monastery at Cracow,[45] the only remaining convent among all those suppressed by the occupying forces. She was very much involved in renewing Carmelite life in Poland, both among the nuns and the friars,[46] and so she was looking for suitable men. In Kalinowski, whom she met in the speakroom when he accompanied her nephew in August 1875, she discerned someone sent by divine Providence, and though she did not dare say anything about her wishes to him then, she did find a way to lead him to Carmel. She began a crusade of prayer for Kalinowski's vocation to the Order,[47] and then initiated a correspondence with him. Joseph himself told his family at Vilna: "I have a sign of the mercy and goodness of the Lord, which brought me hope and consolation through people consecrated to him. Gucio's aunt, the Reverend Sister Mary Xavier of Jesus...whom I met only once at the grilles and who hardly knows me, only a few days ago—exactly when I least expected it—sent me the following poem of the seraphic Saint Teresa:

> Let nothing trouble you,
> Let nothing frighten you,
> All is fleeting,
> God alone is unchanging.

Patient endurance
Obtains everything.
Who possesses God
Wants nothing.
God alone suffices."[48]

These words became Kalinowski's motto. Soon after he wrote, "Each day I take strength from Saint Teresa's words about which I wrote to you, my dear parents, in my last letter."[49] These words, in the end, induced him to join the Teresian Carmelites. Again he wrote to his parents on November 4, 1876: "A year ago there came to me, like an echo, a voice from the grilles of Carmel. This voice was clearly addressed to me and I have accepted it; it was a salvific voice from the infinite mercy of God commanding me. I can only exclaim, 'I will sing the mercies of the Lord forever.' The only thing that now remains for me to do is to ask your parental blessing."[50]

In this situation, Joseph asked Augustus's father to release him from his teaching contract because he didn't want to delay the fulfillment of his religious vocation any longer. At the same time he recommended that the task of teaching Augustus be entrusted to a priest. Joseph's proposal was accepted and on July 5, 1887, he left the Czartoryski household and went to Linz in Austria to find the provincial of the Discalced Carmelites.[51]

6. Discalced Carmelite

The last and the longest stage of Kalinowski's life is the thirty years (1877-1907) he lived in the Carmelite monastery. Consenting to the voice that called him to Carmel, Kalinowski entered, ready to work for God within the church. On November 26, 1877, he went to Graz and was clothed in the habit of the Order, receiving at the same time his religious name: Raphael of Saint Joseph. One year later, he made his religious vows and went to Gyor in Hungary to continue his religious formation and to complete his philosophical and theological studies. There on November 27, 1881, he made his solemn profession in the hands of the Superior General of the Order, Father Jerome–Mary Gotti (the future Cardinal), and after that he was sent to Czerna. In Czerna, on January 15 of the following year, in the only Polish Discalced Carmelite monastery remaining from the suppression, he was raised to the priesthood by Albin Dunajewski, Bishop of Cracow. Raphael immediately began to work for the rebirth of the Teresian Carmel in Poland. Highly regarded by his superiors and his fellow religious, he was continually given the office of superior or other areas of responsibility. In May 1882 he was named assistant to the novice master and elected third councilor of the monastery by the community of Czerna. On October 29 of the same year, the Definitory General of the Order named him prior of Czerna. When his three years as prior were completed, the provincial chapter, at Linz on April 25, 1885, named him fourth provincial councilor. In the triennium of 1888–1891 he was once more prior of Czerna, and during 1891–1894 he became founder and first superior of the Wadowice monastery, until again being named prior of Czerna (1894–1897). During the years 1897–1899, he was superior at Wadowice and second provincial councilor. On October 11, 1899, he was given the office of vicar provincial for the Discalced Carmelite nuns in Galicia, and on May 2, 1903, he became second provincial councilor once again. The last provincial chapter of his life was held at the beginning of 1906, when he was chosen prior of Wadowice.

From this rapid survey one can see that Father Raphael was always a protagonist, a *leader,* a man of courageous initiatives that he brought to completion. He placed all his knowledge and his rich experience of life at the service of the church and the Order. He never forgot that in a certain sense he owed his Carmelite vocation to the Carmelite nuns. For this reason he always remained close to their problems and promoted two new foundations: Przemysl (1884) and Leopoli (1888).[52] "He reserved his most solicitous care for the nuns of the Carmelite Order," one biographer wrote, "because in the line of the purest Teresian tradition they were authentic sentinels of prayer in the church, for the good of the whole People of God."[53] This enabled Father Raphael to work out his theology of the religious life, not by writing a thesis on the subject, but by living it himself. In this area there was no separation between life and theory; he believed and taught with his own life. His words were only echoes of his own lived experience, and in this way, even though his words were not always perfect in form, he touched hearts and was persusive. For Raphael religious men and women were simply Christians drawing closer to Christ. He anticipated—as is characteristic of saints—the affirmations of the Second Vatican Council by connecting religious consecration with baptismal consecration, and by demonstrating how the first is nothing beyond the second except its explicitation and radicalization.[54]

Even if he was initially considered inadequate for such a task, Father Raphael (encouraged by the nuns and above all by the Superior General, Jerome Gotti) became the restorer of the Polish Carmel, fully satisfying all the trust they placed in him. Above all he promoted the foundation of the Wadowice monastery with its "little college," still in existence, where young boys who manifest signs of a religious vocation are formed and instructed.[55] Before his death, efforts were under way to construct a monastery at Cracow, a foundation very dear to his heart, even though, prophetically, he did not favor the site chosen for the monastery.[56]

In his desire to restore the Polish Carmel, Father Raphael was aware that it was not enough to assemble and form vocations and found new convents, but that it was also necessary to recover the heritage of the past. And if it were impossible to return to the province's old monasteries, which had been suppressed and transformed into prisons, offices, and depots, one must at least restore the spirit of the Order. So with great zeal he began researching the conventual archives that had scattered during the suppressions. He recovered a great number of documents regarding the history of individual convents and monasteries and, helped by the nuns, he was able to publish the *Chronicles* of the convents of Vilna, Leopoli, and Warsaw, adding some extracts from the *Chronicles* of monasteries of the friars.[57] Athough these are not professional historiography, he was aware that *historia vitae magistra est* [history is a teacher of life]. Convinced that the future of the Polish Carmel could be constructed only on the foundations of the past, he unquestionably accomplished this goal. Father Honorat Czeslaw Gil, one of the scholars of the history of the province, affirmed that Raphael has contributed immensely to the "construction of bridges uniting the old Province...with the new one erected in 1911."[58] Besides the

Chronicles he published various additional works that recalled other events and the most celebrated figures of the former Polish Carmel.[59] He wished to make Carmel known, to propagate the spirituality of the Order[60] to a wide audience, convinced that in this way it would be possible to root Carmel in Polish areas. He wanted to offer Carmel's treasures to many people, and so he transformed the conventual churches at Czerna and Wadowice into true and proper shrines (the first to Our Lady of Mount Carmel, the second to Saint Joseph) where there were always long lines of people waiting to go into the confessionals to celebrate the Sacrament of Penance. The influx of the faithful from every part of Poland, especially Silesia, was truly spectacular.[61] The Saint also organized communities of the Secular Order of Carmel and also Confraternities of the Scapular of Our Lady of Mount Carmel. He was interested in founding a Carmelite Congregation for women in the active life, but the idea did not find much support from the episcopal curia.[62] He strongly propagated devotion to the Carmelite scapular and was highly esteemed as a confessor and spiritual director of all kinds of people. He was a man ever open to friendship, which is documented by the cordial correspondence he kept with his comrades in the Siberian exile until his death. He was a tireless apostle of union between the churches and as such is venerated in the liturgy.[63]

His earthly career came to a close in the fall of 1907 at Wadowice, while he was still prior of the monastery. He suffered greatly during the last months of his life, exhausted by sickness and work. But it was really at Wadowice that he spent the most beautiful days of his life, seeing the fruits of his labor and dedicating himself to the spiritual direction of many faithful who approached him, even young college students and the clergy of the area. And here, when he became unable to move about anymore, he worked at a table and by writing his *Memoirs* was able review his whole life and prepare himself for his meeting with Christ in death. He notes, in a letter to his friend Father Nowakowski, "Tomorrow is November 2, the day of the faithful departed. When I was still a boy, I dreamed I would die on All Souls Day. Whether I die on that day or not, no matter what happens, I still confess it is always good. Then I salute you cordially, and I ask you, come what may, to say a *De Profundis* for my soul."[64]

Father Raphael did not actually die on November 2, though his dream did, in fact, come true. He died on November 15 (1907), the day when the Carmelite Order, following its own liturgical calendar, remembers all the deceased brothers and sisters of the Order, pleading with God the Father to grant them citizenship with the saints, together with the Blessed Virgin Mary, in the heavenly Jerusalem.[65]

Andrew Kalinowski (1805–1878),
father of Raphael Kalinowski

Our Lady of Ostra Brama (Vilna)
Raphael Kalinowski had great devotion to Mary
under this title.

Kalinowski (standing, second from right) and his companions at the Military Academy in St. Petersburg

Joseph Kalinowski in Siberia (1864)

Letter written by Kalinowski from Usole, Siberia

Dated 31 December — 12 January 1866

Kalinowski (seated, first on the left)
with a group of Polish exiles in Usole, Siberia (1866)

Joseph Kalinowski after his return from exile

Joseph Kalinowski at the Hôtel Lambert in Paris,
where he served as tutor to Prince Augustus ("Gucio") Czartoryski

Discalced Carmelite monastery in Czerna, where Raphael Kalinowski was ordained in 1882 and where he served as prior for many years

St. Raphael of St. Joseph (Kalinowski)
Photo taken on March 30, 1897

Discalced Carmelite monastery founded
by Raphael Kalinowski in 1899 at Wadowice
(birthplace of Pope John Paul II)

St. Raphael Kalinowski's tomb in chapel of Discalced Carmelite monastery in Czerna

II. Elements of His Spirituality

Contemplation and action, action and contemplation, contemplation *in* action, action *that becomes* contemplation—the balance between these two elements of life, as difficult to attain on the psychological as on the theological level, constitutes a particular characteristic of Raphael Kalinowski's personality. Here is a man whom his contemporaries regarded as the incarnation of prayer and whom they even called a "living prayer,"[1] but who was at the same time dedicated to works that were both very demanding and often distracting. Humble, recollected, smiling, he gave the impression of being continually present to the mystery of the living God. His colleagues at the University of Petersburg noticed it, as did the technicians who planned the Kiev-Odessa railroad with him, the Polish insurrectionists against Russian domination, and finally his companions in misfortune in Siberia.[2] Wherever he was, his life was marked by listening to the Word, which led him to a generous response.

1. Contemplative in Action

Joseph Kalinowski wanted to be a lowly man, to disappear among others, to vanish into the crowd, but he didn't succeed in doing so because he was a leader. He was someone who commanded respect with a word, a glance, and above all with his life. Everyone noticed that his life was really prayer—but prayer that was not used as an excuse to omit other things, as sometimes happens. Rather, the opposite was true: prayer impelled him to serve others, to share what little he had. For him prayer was something essential: "The world can deprive me of everything," he says in a letter from Siberia, "but there will always remain a hidden place it cannot reach: prayer. In it, the past, present, and future can be drawn together in hope. O God, what a great treasure you grant to those who hope in you!"[3]

A *leader*, a man who immediately becomes a protagonist every-where: as soon as he is promoted to captain in the Russian Army, he is put in charge of a military fortress; as soon as he asks to resign and lays down his uniform, he is named War Minister, this time against Russia; arrested and condemned to exile, he becomes a moral au-thority, a spiritual support for those unfortunates who quickly elect him as their head and judge, and who pray to the Lord that their freedom be returned through the merits of Joseph Kalinowski.[4] In reality the years of deportation in Siberia were years not only of pain but also of grace: pain changed into grace, a grace bringing him to fuller maturation in the spiritual life, a grace that in the end led him to Carmel—not as if to something new but as if to the promised land, to the desert of love where God awaited him. That is why he was at home in Carmel from the very first day.[5] Even in Carmel he immediately became a *leader*, a protagonist, the restorer of the Pol-ish province after the suppression. He knew how to do it, he had his own secret for ordering everything: prayer. He knew that the big-gest and most difficult problems are resolved on one's knees. Thus he did and desired others to do, the friars, nuns, and laity who en-trusted themselves to his spiritual direction. "We are attracted by activity," he wrote a nun "and they are very few who realize the im-portance of prayer, seeing that Martha asked for help from Mary, not Mary from Martha."[6] He was convinced that forming true Chris-tians was the same as forming individuals disposed to constant prayer, followed up by generous activity; to prayer that leads to ac-tion and to action that becomes contemplation. All this was a reality he first lived out himself.

2. Precursor of the Apostolate of the Laity

On the day he took the Carmelite habit, Joseph Kalinowski was 42 years old. He was ordained a priest at the age of 47. However, from the moment of his *conversion*, which took place with his con-fession on August 15, 1863 (he was then not yet 30), he can be con-sidered a true and genuine apostle, in today's sense of the lay apostolate.[7] From the moment of this confession, Joseph not only oriented his own life toward God, but sought to help others live

Christianity fully. He exerted his apostolic influence first of all on his family members (parents, brothers, sisters), then friends, lost men and women met on the road of his own life, and, above all, very many young people.

Even though it would be interesting to analyze in detail Joseph's apostolic work toward his own family,[8] we would rather dwell on work directed toward the young and other people. We can thereby see a greater proof, I believe, of Kalinowski's apostolic zeal, one not dependent on the ties of love stemming from the bonds of blood, but rooted deeply in the evangelical love of neighbor.

Joseph's educational instinct regarding the young manifested itself while he was still a captain of the military fortress at Brest, where he founded a school for poor and abandoned youth. During the trip to Siberia, he lamented the sad fate of the young[9] and began to instruct some of them, a task he undertook more fully at Usole, adding even religious instruction to the lessons.[10] How seriously he took it is clear: he postponed his departure from that place of punishment because he wanted to finish the children's preparation for First Holy Communion.[11]

Transferred to Irkutsk, he became a co-worker with Father Christopher Szwernicki, the parish priest for the whole of Siberia, becoming a teacher in the parish school.[12] And even though he was an exile and therefore very poor, Joseph took care of an orphan boy, sharing his room and food with him, but especially becoming a friend and teacher—or rather, a father—to him.[13] As a father he worked with Marcin (the boy's name), as a father he instructed him, and as a father he brought him to the sacraments.[14] When the young lad was provided for and began his studies in a school,[15] Joseph found another boy, Francis, with whom he also shared everything he had.[16] In addition, he took a special interest in the welfare of two other orphans, though he was not in a position to help them as he would have liked.[17]

Kalinowski assumed similar commitments, especially the religious instruction of young people, even at Smolensk, where he spent the last stage of his exile.[18] Above all, however, he is known as an educator because of his position as Augustus Czartoryski's tutor. In the process of the prince's education, Kalinowski strongly emphasized two elements: the human and the religious. He rejoiced every time his pupil approached the sacraments, although he gave Augustus suitable freedom,[19] and when Kalinowski had to leave, he proposed that his place be entrusted to a priest who could foster the integral development of the young prince in a more complete manner.[20] Right from the start, Kalinowski had noted that Gucio lacked normal human relationships with his peers, and therefore recommended a school for him. Unfortunately, the prince's illness prevented this from happening.[21]

As for his friends and others for whom Joseph performed the works of an apostle or good samaritan, we don't know them all. He knew how to raise the needy from desperation. Exiles, oppressed by a deep longing for their native land and family, often went mad; suicides were not rare. Joseph and another companion used to take care of the dying, attend the most needy, and offer material aid, sharing what he received from his family. He wrote to his family in Vilnius: "Don't forget that I am ready to suffer any difficulty because God's grace will not abandon me. I have within myself this treasure that nothing can rob me of, nor increase by offering me material goods. Conversely, material poverty brings some people to moral decline. I am thinking especially of these when I ask you for financial help."[22]

This is typical of Kalinowski's reasoning: moral goods are above material ones, and the good of others is above our own. Another incident demonstrates this: Joseph decided to send a symbolic gift to his father from Siberia—a package of his favorite kind of fresh green tea. On the way to buy it, he ran into Ignatius Olszanski, a Lithuanian deportee, who had lost weight and was half-sick, in a miserable state. Kalinowski gave Ignatius the money intended for his father's tea, and excused himself thus in a letter to his family: "I sacrificed your pleasure and my desire, giving to this true Lazarus the amount equivalent to the tea, thinking that God can content you with a greater solace from the fount of his grace and will accept with benevolence this little sacrifice of ours."[23]

With deep sorrow Kalinowski noted the religious indifference among many of his companions in misfortune in Siberia. Not all were Catholics. We see among them Henry Wohl (a Jew from Warsaw), Apollo Hofmeister (a Protestant), Benedict Dybowski, and

Felix Ziemkowicz (both indifferent to religion). Kalinowski strove to help each of them. He distributed the religious books he received from his family and from Mrs. Mlocka, hoping that these would help them rediscover and live their faith. At the same time he was full of esteem and respect for all. He never got involved in the strong and sometimes offensive arguments, thinking that "reasoning, advice, and long speeches often worsen the situation. The only tactic to follow in these cases is the example of St. Monica, and God alone will do the rest."[24] Accordingly he would ask his family: "Recommend in your prayers those who do not believe. They are not lacking in Usole."[25]

Everyone noticed Joseph's attitude. He commanded respect by his demeanor, which proved the best way to attract others to the true faith. Apollo Hofmeister embraced the Catholic *Credo* several years later; Felix Ziemkowicz turned to God and reconciled himself with the church; Benedict Dybowski left the most beautiful testimonial to Father Raphael that we know;[26] Joseph Wasilewski, saved from despair by Kalinowski, entered the Jesuits and then helped the Saint promote the scapular in Romania.[27] The examples are more than sufficient to demonstrate how really fruitful is the apostolate, if it flows abundantly from the font of a truly Christian life. Through the voice of the most recent ecumenical council, Vatican II, the church invites—even more, "calls and obliges"[28]—all the lay faithful to such an apostolate, always and everywhere profitable, indeed, the only one fitting and possible in some circumstances. Our saint can be a model and a patron for them.

3. Extraordinary Confessor and Spiritual Director[29]

From the moment of his youthful conversion, Joseph Kalinowski had a deep appreciation for frequent confession and spiritual direction. Sent into exile, he immediately missed them: "I need spiritual advice," he was to write during his journey to Siberia. "The lack of a confessor like Father Feliciano is a great loss to me."[30] Three months later, he again took up the same subject: "My thoughts return to my last confession, made while still in freedom and memorable to me for the advice of Father Feliciano. As often as

I was at his confessional, an equal number of times my spirit received great light; I am still drawing from this deposit."[31]

We find similar thoughts in many other letters of the Saint.[32] He recalled his confessor in Vilnius and tried to live according to his counsel.[33] He appreciated the advice and submitted to the ministry of the priests he found in Siberia, and helped them in the formation of others.[34] He advised friends and acquaintances to seek help in the Sacrament of Reconciliation,[35] and many found in him, although not yet a priest, a reference point in their spiritual development.

It is as a Carmelite, however, that Kalinowski revealed himself as an extraordinary spiritual director and confessor. The confessional became the privileged place of his work. Witnesses' depositions during the canonization process revealed that, when receiving penitents, he felt himself to be a treasury of divine mercy. He was like a father; he said to everyone "my child, my dear child" and he received penitents full of affection, gentleness, compassion and, at the same time, zeal.[36] It is not surprising, therefore, that his confessional was already crowded in the early hours of morning. "His care in spiritual assistance," observed a penitent, "was extraordinary. At every hour of the day and at every call, he was ready to go down to his confessional. All of this was founded on a deep love of God, to which he clung, and he saw the image of God in every human being."[37]

Raphael Kalinowski was a confessor and spiritual director of many different types of people: men and women religious, priests, family members, friends in exile, lay people of different social classes. He had received from the Lord a very special charism to guide souls on the way to perfection. His confessional witnessed numerous conversions.[38] A Discalced Carmelite nun testifies: "I had been a nun for more than twenty years, but I must confess that only when I confided myself to the spiritual direction of Father Raphael did I begin something like a second novitiate, changing my life radically."[39]

Besides the testimony of others, we can gather indications of how the Saint appreciated the Sacrament of Reconciliation and spiritual direction from a conference he gave to the Discalced

Carmelite nuns of Leopoli.[40] Anticipating the postconcilar liturgical reform, he recovered the full meaning of the sacrament, inasmuch as he was against calling it simply *confession*.[41] For him the Sacrament of Reconciliation "is the baptism of the infinite mercy that we can approach so often, thanks to God's immense goodness."[42] At the same time he feared that the frequent reception of the sacrament might become simply a habit or spiritual pastime.[43] "Sometimes just the desire to free ourselves from the weight that oppresses our soul spurs us to the confessional..., rather than the wish to make ourselves pleasing to God."[44] What counts is not so much tears and long lists, but "the firm resolve to improve that is the touchstone of true contrition. It goes beyond sorrow and displeasure for the fault committed and abhors the sin greatly."[45] The fruits of a good confession are these: "it purifies, heals, fortifies, and beautifies the soul."[46] Strictly necessary, particularly for a scrupulous person, is total obedience to the confessor, who should not be changed often. Frequent and overly long general confessions are not opportune. It is harmful to repeat confessions, returning one's thoughts continually to the past; this would show a serious lack of trust in divine mercy. The Sacrament of Reconciliation is precisely "the invention of divine love."[48] This love had its zenith at the moment of Jesus' death on the cross. From a sense of guilt, contrition is born in us, whose greatest degree is love; and from love is born the desire to be compassionate with Christ, to suffer with him, completing in our own body what is lacking in the sufferings of his Mystical Body, the church.[49] Our saint invited his penitents to such a love, educating them to this *sentire cum ecclesia,* without which he could not imagine being able to live: "In the misery of my life, what would I have become if I had not opened the treasures of your church, O good Redeemer?"[50] As a model of this co-redemptive love, alive and working in the church, he pointed to the figure of the Blessed Virgin Mary: growth in intimacy with her was for Kalinowski the yardstick of progress on the way of perfection, a visible sign of the action of the Holy Spirit.[51] According to the common faith of the church, the Virgin participates in a very special way in the process of the purification of souls, until they are completely stripped of the "old man" and clothed with the armor of the "new man."[52]

4. Apostle of Church Unity

During the preparation of the document *De cultura Ordinis,* which the Teresian Carmel issued after the General Chapter of 1985, there were many comments like: "Our Carmelite heritage obliges us to live and share our values.... The ecumenical dimension of today's problems gives us a special responsibility. In this, Blessed Raphael can be an example."[53]

Truly, our Saint had a very special insight into the ecumenical problem: "Sacred unity! Holy union!" he himself wrote in the essay, already mentioned, that he presented at the Marian Congress of Leopoli in 1904. "Surely this same word fills the heart with sorrow, but at the same time lights the flame of hope."[54] Immediately he adds: "It will be the Immaculate Virgin who will incline the people, in whose breasts beat many noble hearts desirous of peace, toward this union."[55]

Joseph Kalinowski experienced the drama of the division of the church even from his youth. In his native Vilnius, and later more strongly at Brest, he noted the sad fate of Latin Catholics and Uniates, discriminated against by the Czarist power when compared with the Orthodox Church. In his *Memoirs* he often laments this division,[56] which, in a letter, he called the greatest enemy of society.[57] For him, "the safest way to find peace is precisely in union."[58] Elsewhere he confessed that "he couldn't free himself from a deep, interior desire to see Moscow converted."[59] He entered Carmel to serve Christ and to work for the unity of his church.[60] In fact, he did work for it, and despite the increasing weight of years and his steadily weakening health, this was his one consolation: "Please pray for me," he asked a French Carmelite nun, "so that the Lord will grant me above all the grace to love suffering and to persevere on this road. Even if I now feel myself to be declining—I am, in fact, 62 years old—I cannot free myself of the thought that the good God, if I remain faithful to him, will still allow me, with his grace, to work for the unity of the church through the Carmel of our Lady."[61]

With this aim, in 1896 he visited the metropolitan of the Uniates in Leopoli, Archbishop Sylvester Sembratowicz, with whom he discussed the possibility of founding some eastern rite Carmelite convents and monasteries that could later become the nucleus for union.[62] Similarly, through acquaintances he wanted to found a convent of Discalced Carmelite nuns in Bucharest, Romania. Even though his dream could not be realized, with the support of the bishop of Bucharest our Saint succeeded in spreading devotion to the Scapular of Carmel throughout the entire Romanian diocese. This bore much fruit in the ecumenical field: even the Orthodox faithful were asking for Mary's garment while, at the same time, embracing the Catholic *Credo*.[63] With the same intention he sent scapulars also to Siberia and Bulgaria because it was "impossible to free himself of the thought [of union]. And all through Mary! Not only Romania, even Russia!"[64]

Our saint was convinced that unity between the Catholic and Orthodox Churches could be effected through Marian devotion, so alive in both traditions. One certainly cannot disregard this Spirit-inspired intuition. The Virgin Mary brought forth Jesus Christ, one, only and indivisible, Lord of the cosmos and of history, head of the one and indivisible Mystical Body, the Way, the Truth, and the Life of all Christians. Would it not be useful to recall this in every ecumenical speech and to return to the beginnings of our redemption, to the Virgin of Nazareth and, by means of her, filled the Spirit, to find again the lost unity?[65]

Father Raphael also nourished a great devotion to St. Josephat, martyr of unity. In several letters Raphael recalled that saint's personality and martyrdom and invited his brothers and sisters in Carmel, family members, and friends to work for the cause of union of the churches, following St. Josephat's example.[66]

Besides the Orthodox, our saint also desired to see Protestants united in the same church. In a conference he invited the [Carmelite] tertiaries of Wadowice to pray for them and for all Christians cut off from full communion with the Church of Rome.[67] Elsewhere he recalled the return of some from Arianism to the Latin Church.[68] Later, he himself helped the priest Zenon Kwiek, one of the pillars of the Mariavite heresy, to abandon the path of error. In 1906 this priest, after a long talk and confession with Father Raphael, reconciled himself with the church and returned to his diocese.[69] Before that, the Saint received his sister-in-law Helen (wife of his brother

Gabriel), who belonged to the Calvinist reform,[70] into full communion with the Roman Catholic Church, and also Helen's sister
Wanda.[71]

In light of all this, we cannot be surprised that the Opening
Prayer of the Mass of Saint Raphael Kalinowski in the Carmelite Missal (and in the missal for the Catholic Church in Poland), prays to
God "who filled Saint Raphael with an extraordinary ardor of charity for the unity of the church, to grant us, by his intercession, the
grace to be able to collaborate in the unity of all the faithful in
Christ."

5. Forerunner of Vatican II's Theology of Religious Life

In the *Decree on Renewal of Religious Life*, the Second Vatican
Council has reminded us that religious, by professing the evangelical counsels, have placed their entire life at the service of God: "This
constitutes a special consecration, which is deeply rooted in that of
baptism and expresses it more fully."[72] Years earlier, Saint Raphael
had defined the essence of religious life in a similar manner: "Such
is the substance of life in the Order…, in which that first seed of the
life of the spirit—the life we began in God by means of Baptism—is
strengthened, perfected, and raised to the highest degree, for a religious is merely a Christian who stands closer to Christ."[73]

Of what does this particular consecration that occurs by virtue
of baptism consist, according to Father Raphael? Christians obtain
the gift of faith that opens the way to eternal life, and renounce "the
spirit of darkness and all his works" in order to participate in the
grace won by Jesus Christ, through which they become "true
temples of the Most High"; the human soul, by the power of the
baptismal water, truly becomes a dwelling place of God. In this way
human beings have been given the privilege of divine filiation and,
with it "ineffable brotherhood with Jesus Christ." But baptismal consecration—still following the thought of our saint—ordinarily occurs in infancy. A baby is not capable of consciously participating in
the celebration or of imagining its greatness; such consciousness
awakens in proportion to psychological development and physical
maturation. Despite infidelity to our baptismal promises and human

forgetfulness of our "first love," God mercifully lowers himself, helping his poor creatures because "his love knows no limits, nor can it be diminished in action," not even for humanity's great and continual betrayals. It is precisely this "divine love that precedes our paths as we limp along our crooked ways, reminding us of what we forgot, that reignites the past promises in our hearts. Again, this love speaks to us of the original faith, primordial love, and unparalleled innocence that we regained at the baptismal font.... We are won by eternal Love and appear as if awakened from a deep sleep.... We present ourselves again before the Lord's face, now no longer as babies who must be named by the voice of our godparents, but as noble beings in the maturity of our minds and wills. Now it is we ourselves, as adults, who bring to birth the voice in our soul: I will arise and go to the house of my Father."

"It is precisely in this way," concludes the saint, "that baptism is connected to the religious life, to religious consecration. In baptism we renounced the spirit of darkness, joining ourselves to the ranks of the servants of Christ. But this happened when our soul was unaware. In religious profession, with God's powerful assistance, we offer other new promises to be observed more strictly, more diligently, with greater stability, as is proper to the mature age of the spirit that God's grace has predisposed, time has developed, and firm trust in God's mercy has effectively reinvigorated."[74]

Saint Raphael does not make a substantial distinction between baptismal promises and those of religious profession. They are different in subject, but in content and goal they are the same: the person declares war on all that can cause estrangement from Christ. One begins a struggle to live in fraternal friendship with him (in "brotherhood," says the saint literally).

Herein we find the duty of every Christian, that is, of every baptized person: to tend to perfection by faithfulness to the commandments, especially the commandment of love from which all the others flow. Saint Raphael many decades ago emphasized precisely what, in our day, we heard affirmed at the Council: there is a universal vocation to perfection, to holiness, that is rooted in baptism. Every Christian must tend toward and reach it. The identical task, continues our saint, derives also from religious vows: "I constantly remind you of it, so that you don't forget that the task you have undertaken by means of the vows is none other than the effort to tend toward perfection, that is, toward union with God."

In Saint Raphael Kalinowski's view, the religious vocation appears not as something above, nor even next to, the Christian vocation; rather, it is precisely the same vocation as every Christian's, perfectly lived, and made explicit by profession of the evangelical counsels.[75]

6. Mary Always and in Everything

During the special congress of the Congregation for the Causes of Saints that met on March 18, 1980, to discuss Raphael Kalinowski's heroic virtues, the first "relator" recalled in his vote the deep Marian devotion of the Servant of God, evoking his maxim, "Mary always and in everything."[76] The Virgin Mary clearly played a very special role in the saint's life and occupies a unique place in his spirituality.[77] His Marian spirituality corresponds fully to the directives the Council offered us sixty years after the death of the saint. Contemporary Mariology, following the direction Vatican II marked out, emphasizes Mary's greatness as mother of Christ and supereminent member and mother of the church. The theology of our times, therefore, treats the figure of the Blessed Virgin Mary in a christological and ecclesiological context.[78] Saint Raphael Kalinowski's Mariology had such an orientation. His Marian spirituality does not stop with the figure of Mary, but through her leads to Christ, living and working in the church, his Mystical Body. Let us briefly review the principal aspects of this spirituality:

1. His conversion took place after college on account of *Mary,* and led Joseph Kalinowski to *Christ* through the sacramental ministry of the *church;*[79]

2. His entrance into Carmel, the order of *Mary,* had as its goal to serve *Christ* more closely and to work for the unity of his *church;*[80]

3. The testimony of a religious life in imitation of *Mary*—"the Book where the eternal Word of God, *Christ the Lord,* is read to the world"[81]—is confirmed and blessed by the *church;*

4. Fidelity to the religious vocation of the *Brothers [and Sisters] of the Blessed Virgin Mary* does not consist of a sentimental love for her, but in "attending to her affairs,"[82] seeing in her the secure guide to *Christ,* in other words:

> • accepting and accomplishing—like her—the will of God, contemplating and preaching his Word made flesh in *Christ Jesus,* author of our salvation, of which the *church is now the sacrament;*[83]

> • spiritually directing the souls of his brothers and sisters, pointing out to them the road *ad Jesum per Mariam* [to Jesus through Mary] or, better yet, *ad Jesum cum Maria* [to Jesus with Mary], taking as a base the common faith of the *church* in her role as mediatrix of grace until all of the "old man" is stripped off and they put on the armor of the *"new man";*[84]

> • propagating the scapular devotion—a sign of salvation and the *Mother's* gift—a sacramental of the *church* that helps sanctify every moment of life and attain the salvation accomplished by *Christ.*[85]

In the final analysis, *Mary always and in everything,* but inasmuch as she guides us to *Christ* and brings us to communion with him in his *church,* "to make us living stones of this church, willing servants of our brothers and sisters on this earth and, after death, participants in God's glory forever."[86]

III. Selections from the Saint's Works

The Church Is Our Home*

(Conference delivered to the members of the Secular Order in Wadowice, March 29, 1893, on the occasion of the festivities for the twenty-fifth anniversary of the pontificate of Leo XIII)

1. In Poland there used to be a saying, "You can feel good anywhere, but in your own home you feel better." I think we can understand this saying in a more extended sense. Actually the whole world is our home, wherever human beings live, all of them unconditionally created in the image and likeness of God. The sky full of stars is beautiful, a day when the sun shines is certainly beautiful, everything in nature is beautiful, but certainly God himself is the most beautiful; consequently, the most beautiful creature is the human being, whose soul was made in the image of the divine beauty. Hence, you can feel good everywhere, but better in the home of your own soul.

2. Then, out of this immense whole comprising all humanity, a great number of persons is gathered who together make up, under the leadership of the pope, the holy church. She is our second home.

3. Jesus has said of the church that the gates of hell will not prevail against it [Mt 16:18], and that he himself will be with us until the end of the world [cf. Mt 28:20]. To Peter he even said, "Your are Rock, and upon this rock I will build my church" [Mt 16:18]. In the church, Jesus himself is present in the Blessed Sacrament. She is governed by his vicar, the Holy Father, that is to say, the pope. To

---

* *Section numbers in the four selections from the Saint's works are those of the Polish editor, P. Czeslaw Gil.*

39

him Jesus gave the keys of the kingdom of heaven and conferred on him the power to forgive or not to forgive sins [cf. Mt 16:19].... To the church Jesus entrusted the sacraments and all the other spiritual helps for the faithful; he gave us the Blessed Virgin as mediatrix, the holy angels as guardians and companions, so that we might be able to free ourselves from sin and rise to new life....

4. Therefore, if on occasion we happen to hear reference made to schismatics, heretics, evangelicals, protestants, etc., who are separated from us and consequently cannot fully benefit from the gifts bestowed on the church by the Lord...let us pray for them, and for all those who do not belong to the church, that one day they may be able to enter it....[1]

Let us reproach ourselves for the ingratitude, negligence, and inconstancy in our own response to so many graces...and let us promise to correct ourselves in the future. And in moments of doubt let us cry out, "I believe in everything the church proposes to us for our belief." In a word, in the difficulties of life and in the moments when we are tempted to go after false goods, let us hold fast to the bark of Peter, which is for us like Noah's ark at the time of the deluge, since we feel good everywhere but better in the House of God, where everything is done according to his will. In this house Jesus is with us until the end of the world.

5. The visible head of this house, of this (if you will) bark of Peter, ark of the covenant, is the pope; the invisible head is Jesus himself. To holy church all the peoples of the earth hasten, insofar as all the nations...will find a refuge in it. Our Redeemer, ever present in the Most Blessed Sacrament, extends his hands to everyone. He opens his heart and says, "Come to me, all of you" [Mt 11:28].

Thus he calls and invites us, so that there might be one shepherd and one flock! Today's solemnity of the twenty-fifth jubilee of the pontificate [of Leo XIII] is, therefore, celebrated simultaneously throughout the world: in Wadowice, in Moscow (where there are in fact Catholic churches), in Germany, England, America, and wherever the church is present....

6. In the church the Holy Father is infallible in matters of faith and morals. The Holy Father appoints bishops, who ordain priests,

and approves and establishes religious congregations. Through the pastors of the church, all of us receive the truth of the faith, and thus there is created a unity between us here present and the Holy Father. And if we obey the pope, we obey the Lord Jesus, according to his own words addressed to Peter and the other apostles: "Whoever hears you, hears me" [Lk 10:16].

7. Therefore, we have the duty to assist the pope, and if we are unable to do it in other ways, let us help with prayers and good works. Let us seek to accomplish with all possible perfection and with the gift of ourselves all the actions of our daily life, even the most insignificant. Let us offer them to the Lord in sacrifice; let us elevate all that we do to a supernatural level, seeking to walk always in the presence of God. In so doing we shall truly belong to the soul of the church, and therefore even the simplest things will be transformed into the sublime; our renunciations and sacrifices, made for the love of God and neighbor, will increase the holiness of the church. With an exemplary Christian life, keeping in mind that we Carmelites belong to the Order of the Blessed Virgin Mary, let us willingly make ourselves living stones of the church, willing servants of our brothers [and sisters] on this earth, so that we can, after our death, participate in the glory of God forever.

On a Good Confession

*(Conference given at the monastery of the Discalced Carmelite nuns in Leopoli for the
feast of St. John of the Cross, November 24, 1902)*

1. When we wish to draw fruit from the celebration of a saint's
feastday, our mind is accustomed to roam here and there, seeking
in this saint's life the flower in which to taste the most substantial
nourishment.

In the crown of virtues adorning the life of our Holy Father
John of the Cross, so abundant in every kind of fragrant flower, what
other virtue could we focus upon more profitably than that rare
purity of heart, detached from everything earthly, flooded with God
alone, desiring to suffer and be despised out of love for his savior,
and, by that very fact, open to whatever could make of him an altar
for a continual self-immolation?

2. Indeed, what else should our heart be? It should be the altar of God: "Dei altare cor nostrum" [St. Augustine, *De civitate Dei*,
X, 3, 2]. *Humilis corde, Cor Christi est;* those who are humble of heart,
make themselves like the heart of Christ.

Upon our heart the offerings are placed, and the sacrifice is
offered; within it is the most intimate sanctuary, the most secret
place, the dwelling where the Holy of Holies reposes. "We will come
to him and make our dwelling with him" [Jn 14:23]. "I will enter his
house and dine with him and he with me" [Rv 3:20].

This indwelling of God in the soul of the just explains to us
the extraordinary deeds in the lives of the saints. They are in the
world, but as if they were not. They are in the world to carry out a
mission, living a life of love and sacrifice through which God pre-
serves them for himself, but they are not in the world because the
principal reason of their existence is elsewhere: in God, who fills the
soul and in whom it lives absorbed.

For such a life our Holy Father [John of the Cross] prepared
his heart, making it a true altar of the living God; he transformed
himself into our model and today, more than ever, he encourages
us to imitate him.

"Depart with rapid flight from creatures,
Place your desire only in God,
Hide your heart in that of the Savior,
Make your nest in the starry heavens."

3. In old-fashioned paintings, certainly not with the striking colors of today but with a more profound sense that caused the soul's gaze to rise toward God, certain mysteries were depicted showing the Child Jesus as he prepared for himself an agreeable resting place in the human heart.

First the Lord cleanses the heart and pardons its sins; then he heals and puts it in order; later he strengthens the heart so it can be adorned with virtues as with a crown of blessings; finally, he enters and closes the door behind him.

4. He first purifies the heart with the baptism of his most Precious Blood. This baptism of his infinite mercy, this invention of divine love, that we can approach so often, thanks to God's immense goodness, is the sacrament of penance....

In it we prostrate ourselves at the foot of the cross so that, with our tears of repentance, the springs of his most Precious Blood might pour forth from the Savior's heart, and we, alongside the good thief, might confess our sins, trusting that we will obtain pardon and with the hope of being with the savior in paradise. And Jesus himself shuts up our heart so that it will live within him.

5. Normally we use the word "confession" instead of "sacrament of penance" in our ordinary speech. Since the use of this word is so widespread, it is difficult to object to it, but it certainly restricts the meaning of this sacrament.

Likewise, we have called the sacrament of penance—this invention of God's love—a "sacrament of the dead." A priest once said to a pious woman: "My daughter, do you want your soul to come back to life, your failings to disappear, those failings which make you turn back from your resolutions and displease you, causing you restlessness and complaints? Go to confession frequently and confess well. Do you want to carry out with a generous heart your obligations, at times too heavy and contrary to your disposition? Do you want the strength to keep yourself from losing heart when suffering comes upon you? Go to confession frequently, and confess well.

Lastly, if you want to be holy and walk quickly on the road to heaven, go to confession frequently and confess well!"

6. We are all convinced of this truth, but so is the enemy of our souls who, knowing the fruits of good confessions, uses every possible effort to destroy these fruits as soon as they appear.

First he uses ourselves, later he acts alone; he enkindles in us the desire to be satisfied only with the flowers, and extinguishes [awareness of] the necessity of working to gather the fruits as well. To do this, he travels the path that we ourselves open to him, because God is not always the only [motive]...when we go to confession. Sometimes it is primarily or solely the desire to free ourselves from the weight that oppresses our soul, and so to ease our conscience, that spurs us to the confessional, rather than the wish to make ourselves pleasing to God. All this happens because we seek only our personal satisfaction. The Evil One is not troubled by devout sighs, by torrents of soft tears and afflictions of the heart, when all of this substitutes for the awareness of the duties of our state in life, when it relegates to oblivion fidelity to most sacred obligations, when it excludes the resolution not to act in the future against our own conscience. We go to confession more out of habit than to confess ourselves well.

"What frightens me above all," said a person of exemplary life before dying, "are my confessions made out of habit, without due care in preparing myself for repentance." We go to confession like those debtors who go to settle an account; they pay, but with no intention to avoid contracting a new debt. They want to appear as persons of their word, but they do this so they can receive new loans from their creditors.

7. A firm purpose of amendment is the touchstone of true repentance. It goes much further than mere sorrow or affliction over a mistake one has committed. It reinforces our hatred for sin, projecting it toward the future with a resolute decision not to repeat our sin nor to offend God with it.

8. Those who sincerely repent out of love observe that, although this is enough to obtain absolution, they do not rest satisfied at heart because of it. Much has been pardoned them, because they love much [cf. Lk 7:47]; but the fear remains that, after the dew of the Divine Blood has made the field of his soul fruitful again, this

field, perhaps by lack of careful cultivation, could change from fruitful to desert ground.
The soul already knows its condition. It owes its salvation to
divine mercy alone: "Misericordiae Domini, quia non sumus
consumpti" [It is through the mercy of God that we have not been
destroyed (Lam 3:22)]. The fear of a possible rupture in its covenant
with God takes hold of the soul. Therefore, purifying its sins in the
sacrament of penance, through the merits of the blood shed for it,
the soul exercises itself in this degree of repentance, where fear and
love join hands.
9. In this degree of perfection God still hides himself from the
soul's view, but the soul doesn't rest from climbing still higher. At
the foot of the cross, seeing its savior drink the bitter chalice to the
very dregs, solely out of love for her, seeing him immolate himself
for her sins, the soul dissolves with love for him, sheds tears of grati-
tude, and wants to hide herself forever in his most sweet Heart. With
this love it no longer desires anything else, only to suffer or die, to
suffer and be despised, to be truly in its own life what is signified in
the subtitle of our Holy Father: "of the Cross." Having loved much,
much is forgiven her [cf. Lk 7:47].

> Living on Love is banishing every fear,
> Every memory of past faults.
> I see no imprint of my sins.
> In a moment love has burned everything....
> Divine Flame, O very sweet Blaze!
> I make my home in your hearth.
> In your fire I gladly sing:
> "I live on Love!..." [2]

10. As the raging sea seems to feel displeasure at all that pol-
lutes it, and desires to expel from itself anything foreign, so that the
beauty of the mysteries it holds might appear to view in all clarity, so
the soul does not tolerate anything within itself unless it is of God
or leads to God; approaching confession from the abyss of her misery, she casts off everything, desiring to preserve in herself only the
image of God according to which she was created, to look only at
him and to rejoice only in him.

In her love-filled tears she receives a shower of graces that descend from the wounds of her Savior. The misery of sin makes way for grace, the thorns become roses, and even the very poison of sin changes into an antidote for the soul. Here are the fruits of a good confession: it purifies, heals, fortifies, and beautifies the soul.

11. All that we have treated so far leads us back to what we discussed at the beginning: imitating our Holy Father [John of the Cross] by using the means the Savior left us to purify our soul, to preserve the heart ever pure in order to be able to transform it into an altar of the living God, and to become enamored of him in suffering and being despised: *Altare Dei, cor nostrum! Humilis corde, cor Christi est* [The altar of God is our heart; the humble heart is like the heart of Christ].

12. In the sketch of the *Ascent of Mount Carmel* drawn by Our Holy Father John of the Cross, we read: "Here there is no longer any way because for the just...there is no law." This means that if all the prescriptions of the law have as their object the love of God, when this is fully attained, the prescriptions cease of themselves. True repentance, in crushing the heart of man, crushes everything opposed to the love of God and destroys all that does not lead to him.

13. Blessed by our Holy Father! Without knowing a stain on his soul, he managed to arrive at the harbor of eternal happiness! We who still live in dangerous circumstances, guiding the bark of our soul over the waves, across this storm of foaming waters that is our life, insecure, will we be able to reach this harbor?

14. Jesus, hope of suffering humanity, our refuge and our strength, whose light pierces the black clouds that hang over our stormy sea, enlighten our eyes so that we can direct ourselves toward you who are our harbor. Guide our bark with the rudder of the nails of your cross, lest we drown in the storm. With the arms of this cross rescue us from the turbulent waters and draw us to yourself, our only repose, Morning Star, Sun of Justice, for with our eyes obscured by tears, we can catch a glimpse of you there, on the shores of our heavenly homeland. Redeemed by you, we pray: *Salvos nos fac propter nomen tuum*—"save us for the sake of your holy name" (St. Augustine).

And all this through Mary.

Baptism and Religious Vows

(Conference given to the Discalced Carmelite nuns for the renewal of vows, on the occasion of a pastoral visit. Date and place unknown)

1. *"Inveni quem diligit anima mea*—I have found him whom my soul loves" [cf. Song 3:4].

We are assembled here to renew spiritually the memory of a sacred ceremony upon which our temporal and spiritual destiny depends. With this renewal we confirm the vows we once pronounced. That important ceremony of our profession is, in turn, united by a strong bond to an earlier and even more important ceremony that we naturally recall today: the promise made to God in baptism.

2. Still mere infants, we were carried for the first time to the Lord's House. The priest inquired in the name of the church: "What do you ask for?" And standing there were some who, taking charge of our physical and spiritual incapacity, assumed responsibility for us and answered in our name that we asked for the faith that gives eternal life. When the priest continued to inquire in the name of God: "Do you renounce Satan with all his works and pomps?" those same spiritual guardians obligated themselves for us to truly renounce all of this toward the day when the torch of reason, as yet unawakened, might shine in our spirit.

Through the word given by our worthy representatives, and by means of his minister, Christ our Lord washed our soul from original sin with that water which, together with his blood, gushed forth from his pierced side. And he anointed with the holy oils our tiny infant members, just as a bishop does when he blesses a church, so that it might become the dwelling-place of God.

The soul became the true sanctuary of the Most High, we were covered with a white garment, a sacred symbol and magnificent expression of the innocence we regained, a garment of victory and triumph like that worn by those in the kingdom of God who "follow the Lamb wherever he goes" [Rv 14:4].

3. That was a great and solemn moment! And even if we were unable to participate consciously, that ceremony—as always happens—filled all who attended it with joy. Everyone rejoiced, the devout as well as the worldly. And yet, that ceremony was begun with words that sadden this frivolous world, the words "I renounce." These words were transformed into the foundation of our Christian dignity, into the theme of our marvelous fraternity in Christ, into an incentive toward a spiritual life for God and in God, in order that we might thereby recover that privilege we lost through our first parents, the privilege of being children of God and heirs of eternal glory.

What great and fruitful words, but how few there are who can appreciate their sacred value! "I renounce!" We all pronounce this phrase through the mouth of our godparents. With this renunciation we all are inscribed in the list of the confessors of Christ, God and man, who renounced the majesty of eternal glory to share in our misery. With these words we declare war on the world, a tenacious spiritual war, until death. Thus this phrase will always appear harsh and bitter.

For many of us, so much time has already passed since that first ceremony of our Christian life. Other sacred ceremonies have evoked it again, since the church, as a solicitous mother, has continually kept alive in us the memory of our duties toward God, other persons, and ourselves. Nevertheless, despite having promised so much to God, we have quickly forgotten what we promised, and the words "I renounce" have become for us an unbearable offering, words suggesting sadness and affliction.

Why? Because we still find pleasurable all those things whose renunciation would lead us to lasting and authentic happiness.

5. In spite of this, the God of mercy does not cease coming to the aid of his weak creature. The life of human beings and their most ambitious desires have limits, while God's love has none. This love accompanies us along our way, surprises us in our erring wayward paths, and reminds us of what we have forgotten; it repeats in our hearts the promises made on a day long ago, and speaks to us at length of our first faith, of that first charity, of that incomparable innocence regained with holy baptism. A stream of tears floods

one's conscience at the sight of the loss of those treasures, and to this the Spirit of God bears witness. Christ's mercy endures everything, and does not think evil but rejoices in the good; it intercedes for us, and knocks on the door of our heart, it lowers itself until it conquers the soul with its love full of humility.

What Christ accomplished in Judea during the thirty-three years of his earthly life is reproduced in every human heart.

Even still today, right up until death, his love continues to struggle with our egoism. And we see today what results: conquered by eternal love and awakened from a deep sleep, we remember the promises made at holy baptism, raise our eyes to heaven, and present ourselves again before the Lord's face, now no longer as infants who speak through the mouth of others spiritually substituting for them, but as persons mature in their own reason and will. And along with the prodigal son, we say: "How many of my father's hired hands have bread in abundance, while here I die of hunger! I shall arise and go to my father" [Lk 15:17-18]. Again I renounce Satan and all his works and pomps, forever, because, Father, I want to remain beside you forever. It is true that in holy baptism I promised all this, but then I forgot my promise and didn't carry it out. Now I come to your sanctuary so that the memory of your love never depart from me. To not worry any more for the rest of my life, it is enough for me to know that I cross your threshold, for where you are, Lord, there is peace, happiness, and tranquility of heart: "I rejoiced when I heard them say: Let us go to the house of the Lord!" And to this house we have come. *Laetatus sum in his, quae dicta sunt mihi: in domum Domini ibimus* [Ps 121:1].

6. Thus it is easy to understand how closely bound to the ceremony of baptism is our vocation to the Order and therefore the pronouncing of our vows. With the first [i.e., baptism] we renounced the spirit of darkness, joining ourselves to the ranks of the servants of Christ; and this happened in what was also still an infancy of the spirit. With the vocation to the Order, we made, with God's help, other promises that we must observe more strictly, more diligently, with greater stability, as is proper to the mature age of the spirit that God's grace has predisposed, time has developed, and firm trust in God's mercy has effectively reinvigorated.

7. Together with the white garment of baptism, we think of that white veil which covered your eyes during the ceremony of initiation into religious life. It should not be forgotten, but should be regarded the same way as the white garment of innocence received in baptism. For it could happen that, in the hand of the Supreme Judge on the terrible day of Judgment, the white veil of the novice may be matched with the white baptismal garment.

When, later on, the black veil, symbol of the renunciation of the world, was placed upon you, precious texts of the prophet-king[3] were recited, texts speaking in the name of a soul who longs to be united to God: "I had hardly left them [the guards of the city] behind, when I found him whom my heart loves. I held him fast and would not let him go" [Song 3:4]. In these few words is contained the entire life of a soul, its struggles, its desires, its obligations and its reward.

8. Like the Bride in the Canticle with the guards of the city, so the soul "left behind" worldly persons, custodians of vanity. The soul "left them behind" through spiritual recollection, through a greater self-knowledge, through a more attentive consideration of what God requires of us for salvation. The frivolous world doesn't want to know, hear, or think that its vanities can disappear; but when the soul, "leaving it behind," has barely made a few steps in this direction, it sees that the world easily fades from view.

9. It is something remarkable that the world should appear as the sum of all that is great, powerful, and dazzling to the senses, yet all that is needed is to remove oneself from it just a little and all its greatness so diminishes in the eyes of the one who leaves it that it practically vanishes.

It seems then as if it is the world that feels sadness at being abandoned by us, rather than we in abandoning the world. Why? Does the world still fear those who, up until yesterday, were its slaves? No. It is because the world doesn't see us alone on this new road. It sees that Jesus has placed himself alongside us. And on the face of Jesus there is blood, on his brow there is a crown of thorns, and on his shoulders a large and heavy cross. This so terrorizes the world that its weak and dull sight is incapable of perceiving this sweet divine Face that ravishes all those who approach it. As soon as the world sees the crucified one it runs away, astonished, fleeing at the same time from all those who are close to Christ. The Apostle to the Gentiles had already spoken of this from personal experience: "We preach Christ Crucified, folly to the Gentiles" [1 Cor 1:23].

10. And so, dear sisters, by "leaving behind" the custodians of the world's vanity, you have overcome the first difficult obstacle for your own weak nature. What remained to be done in this new way that you have undertaken in life? There remained an ardent desire of your heart to "find" the Lord, the Beloved of the soul; this was your desire: *inveni eum* [I have found him]. Then an even more lively desire arose in your soul, to "hold" the Lord you have found. It was your duty: *et tenui eum* [and I held him]. When, with the strong embrace of your total sacrifice, you helped your Savior and used efficacious means to "keep him" forever in the cell of your heart, *et non dimittam* [and not let him go], it was then that you understood the meaning of the words, "I found him, I held him, I will not let him go." Then you received the reward for your labors, your desires, and the fulfillment of your obligations.

This is the essence of life in the Order: work, love, and sacrifice. With this, religious souls strengthen themselves, perfect themselves, and bring to the highest degree the spiritual life begun in God by means of baptism. For a religious is merely a Christian who stands closer to Christ.

11. With the vow of chastity you have found the Lord, with that of poverty you have assisted him, and with that of obedience you will never lose him.

Voluntary chastity of soul and body is the one thing worthy of "finding" him who was called "the Rose of Sharon and the Lily of the Valley" [Song 2:1], whose mother is the Virgin and whose Father is God. A jealously kept chastity finds Jesus first, reposes more closely to his heart, always listens to its beating, and will respond to him in everything.

Every soul who loves chastity will certainly find him who is the king of chastity. But how will it "hold" him? With what power will it be able to hold him who is the Lord of Majesty, whom heaven and earth cannot contain?

12. Only those live happily who resemble this Lord of glory, who described himself as "meek and humble of heart" [Mt 11:29]. Throughout his entire life he lived with the unfortunate, with

sinners and the poor, earning for himself the name of "a friend of sinners," that is, of the world's poorest. He gave them all that he had, and at the end he died naked on a cross for unfortunate humanity. Thus it is impossible to "hold him" if not through a poverty of one's very self, a voluntary bodily poverty, an ever sincere poverty of spirit. It is necessary all the days of our life to beg in love and humility for the riches that he distributes daily to us through his heart. He refuses only the person who does not wish to admit his own weakness, he sends away only the unhappy proud person. You must "hold him" well and strongly, with a poor spirit, with a poor heart, with a life entirely poor.

13. If through chastity you "find" him, through humility—poverty of spirit—you will "hold him" and conquer him. Will he remain with you always? What a sad question, and how sad is the insecurity of the human heart, always menaced by the danger of its own instability!

The life of a soul who seeks true happiness clearly and indisputably depends on this: that those who seek their joy in God are the ones who give joy to God.

14. This truth impresses us, because we realize that in seeking God as the object our own happiness through the vows we have pronounced, we can in turn please the Creator and Savior of the world; and we become fearful seeing in all its reality the obscuring of the mind caused by the darkness that opposes itself to the truth, and by the indolence of the will in pursuing the end it itself has chosen.

Not seeking God as the sole end of our happiness, and [not seeking] a silent repose in him, the soul's capacities are dissipated; not finding rest, they seek their contentment in the satisfaction of their natural impulses.

By eliminating from our life this truth, that those who seek their satisfaction in God are those who please God, we break that promise made to God in baptism—"I renounce"—and before God we change ourselves in the religious life into lifeless stones that seek peace in him in vain, peace with ourselves and with all that surrounds us.

It is we ourselves who will deprive ourselves of the reward promised by the Savior, by retreating from this divine presence, and forgetting his words: "Where two or three are gathered together in my name, there am I in the midst of them" [Mt 18:20]. Without seeking him, we cannot "find him"; without "finding him" we cannot "hold him"; without "holding him" we cannot "keep him."

The ancient invitation contained in these words, "I found him, I held him, I will not let him go," is changed into nothing, into a dead letter.

15. By describing this aspect of religious life, with its advantages and its dangers, I have tried above all to cement the mutual efforts with which we began this visit,[4] upon the foundation of the truth of our life. *Fundamenta eius in montibus sanctis* [His foundation upon the holy mountain (the Lord loves)] [Ps 86:1].

We entrust our task to our Most Holy Mother, the Virgin Mary, under her maternal care.

If there is anything to correct, let it be corrected once and for all; may the good that is done continue to increase.

Toward this purpose, may God's love flood your souls along this earthy life, and finally lead you to the fountain of love, that is, to God himself in eternity.

Mother of God, Hope of the World

(Conference delivered to the Discalced Carmelite friars in Wadowice, Poland in 1906, on the vigil of the feast of the Mary's Divine Maternity. According to the liturgical calendar of that time, the feast fell on the second Sunday of October. In the margin of the first page of the manuscript, the author noted the date: October 3, 1906.)

1. According to a well-known adage, *non multa, sed multum* [not many, but much]: that is, when we deliberate or reflect on something, we should moderate the number of concepts used. Rather than speculate with *many,* it is better to limit ourselves to a few, in order to attain a *much* greater profundity. In our time, with the tremendous ability no matter where we are to know what is happening almost anywhere on earth, our minds are easily scattered in a thousand directions, and we have difficulty trying to concentrate on what ought to interest and attract us most. In such a situation of inner confusion, those who truly wish to love God and neighbor, to his greater glory and their own spiritual advantage, have a clear source of support: devotion to the Most Holy Virgin.

2. Writing in the middle of the seventeenth century, one of Holy Mother Church's great teachers experienced this personally:

"If it were possible to climb a lofty tower and from there to gaze out over the state of Christianity, we would be able to see a multitude who are believers in name only, hardly different from unbelievers; the divine works treated as fables; our neighbors' misery affecting us so little that it might more properly be said that they are regarded as enemies; the denial of God, the almost universal disregard for justice. What has become of the glorious days of the first believers, at the beginnings of the church?"

"Considering all that has happened," adds the same author, "there is, nevertheless, one fact that stands out against this sad horizon: the ever-increasing fervor in devotion to the Most Holy Virgin, a Marian fervor stronger than that of the finest centuries of Christianity. This could be compared to a seed given by the merciful providence of God, so that in the end humanity might be saved."

3. If a voice made itself heard in this way three centuries ago, the voice of Holy Mother Church in our own time is not very different. In those former times, people took refuge under the protection of the Virgin Mary, Mother of God, who renewed the church. Why shouldn't we, in our own times, also receive help from heaven, if we faithfully invoke Mary in the glory of her Divine Maternity? Celebrating today the feast of the Divine Maternity of Mary, we can obtain, with her powerful intercession, new assistance for a more robust faith.

4. "You ask me," St. Eleutherius says, "what kind of Mother this is. You should have first asked me what kind of Son this is." To measure the greatness of Mary's dignity, constituted by her being mother of God, you would first have to measure, if you had the ability, the dignity involved in being the Son of God. The Divine Maternity of Mary has no other measure than the very infinity of God, because only in that does it find its adequate terminus. The Only-Begotten [Son], who had a life without a beginning in the bosom of God, willed to receive in the bosom of this Mother a new form of life, previously unknown.

Who could measure the degree of exaltation to which this Mother was elevated? Perhaps only God, her Creator, can know totally her dignity and the treasures she possesses.

5. For, in the natural order of things, Mary through her Divine Maternity takes on the closest degree of relationship with God himself, who took a body from her body; furthermore, because she is a virgin, such a degree of consanguinity bestows on Mary the right not only of maternity but also of paternity over Christ. And this relation will last forever.

What shall we say, then, if we contemplate the Mystery of the Incarnation in the light of the grace through which Mary, by a divine decree incomprehensible to human beings, was predestined by God to be without any stain of sin?

6. Just as there is nothing greater than God, says Saint Thomas, so none can attain a higher dignity than the Mother of God. Mary, with her Maternity, is like a book in which the world can read the Eternal Word, Jesus, the Lord.

What can one say of the fullness of grace God bestowed on the Most Holy Virgin, to the limits of his power, giving her a dignity surpassing our capacity to understand? When a wise man was asked "Who is God?" he answered, "If I could define who God is, either God would not exist or I myself would be God." Likewise, to the question "What is it to be the Mother of God?" one can only give a similar answer. "If anyone could comprehend this dignity, either Mary would not be the Mother of God, or the one claiming to understand such greatness would be superior to her whose dignity is immeasurable."

7. For us, Mary became the Mother of all human beings by virtue of her Maternity. In relation to God, the adoration that angels and mortals give her has raised her to an unlimited greatness, for through the Word of God becoming man in her and glorifying God the Father, Mary has brought it about that God, if we may say so, is glorified by God himself.

8. Mary obtained all this by her consent to be Mother, when, invited by the angel, she pronounced those words that resound throughout the ages: "Behold, I am the servant of the Lord, let it be done to me as you say" [Lk 1:38]. What word had the angel addressed to her? These marvelous words: "The Holy Spirit will come upon you and the power of the Most High will overshadow you, for the Child to be born will be called the Son of God" [Lk 1:35].

At the very same moment that Mary said "Let it be done to me according to your word," the Word became flesh [Jn 1:14], and her Divine Maternity became a reality: "She conceived through the power of the Holy Spirit" [Mt 1:18].

9. Three times each day we recite the *Angelus*. This act of piety is but an evocation of that Maternity. It brings to life within us the mystery, accepted only by faith, of the Divine Incarnation's dependence upon Mary's consent. The wood of the cross, through which God redeemed the world, was raised on this consent: "Let it be done to me according to your word." From it flowed the fountain of grace, with it the door to the Kingdom of Heaven, previously closed, was opened. Through it the Savior could become present on our altars, and the marvels of the Virgin Mother of God's mediating power could shine forth; and—for believers who want to profit from what has been done through Mary by the One of whom we read in the

Magnificat, "God who is mighty has done great things in me" [Lk 1:49]—there is outlined the way of imitating the Most Holy Virgin. The "motto" of this imitation is summed up in these few words: "Let it be done to me as you say," that is, in total submission to the will of God, in the state of life to which God has called each of us. Better and more than anyone else, we who are doubly the children of Mary should imitate her, to be enriched as faithful children with the fruits of her maternity; seeking the *unum necessarium*, the one thing necessary for salvation, to steer our life's ship without danger through the hard passage of this world, safe from the disturbances of our times; and finally, obtaining for all of humanity an end to distress and the dawn of light upon the world's horizon.

Notes

NOTES TO PART I

1. J. Kalinowski, *Wspomnienia 1835–1837* [Memoirs 1835–1887], ed. R. Bender (Lublin, 1965). Hereafter cited as M, with page number.

2. Ibid., pp. 3–4.

3. Even his religious vocation itself, his existence as a Carmelite, is nothing but living as radically as possible his own Christian existence: "A religious," he said, "is only a Christian who stands closer to Christ." See R. Kalinowski, *Swietymi badzcie: Konferencje i teksty ascetyszne* [Become Saints: Conferences and Ascetical Texts], ed. Czeslaw Gil (Kracow, 1987) 24, 10; 25, 5. Hereafter it will be cited as C, followed by the number and paragraph of the conference quoted.

4. Karol Wojtyla, former Archbishop of Kracow, said it best when he presented the figure of our Saint this way during a homily preached at Czerna on November 15, 1966, for the celebration of the millennium of Polish Christianity. The Archbishop praised Kalinowski's Polish patriotism, because he accepted even death for the love of his homeland; and he praised him as a model of Christian life, which led him to die for the Eternal God behind monastery walls. For our Italian translation of the discourse, see *Rivista di Vita Spirituale* 36 (1983): 308–313.

5. M 4–5.

6. Ibid., 7–8.

7. Ibid., 8 (note *a*).

8. Ibid., 14.

9. J. Kalinowski, *Listy* [Letters], vol. I, ed. Czeslaw Gil (Lublin, 1978); vol. II, ed. Czeslaw Gil (Krakow, 1985), Letter no. 2. Hereafter these will be cited L, followed by the number of the letter (numbered consecutively across both volumes).

10. M 34.

11. L 8.

12. Cf. M 34.

13. Ibid.

14. L 11.

15. M 55.

16. Ibid., 65.

17. Ibid., 61.

18. L 36.

19. M 67.

20. Here are a few characteristics of Muraviev's regime, as he himself described his goals: "I began with the priests. In one week there were two hangings. People didn't think I was capable of doing this. Nevertheless the people were very fearful.... But our government must be convinced that the first enemy to be fought is the Polish national spirit that is united with Catholicism. Actually Polish and Catholic are synonomous ideas in the language of the people. Limiting any Catholic influence is the first step of our program.... It's necessary to eliminate Catholic monasteries. And we must accomplish the elimination of the Polish language from schools, as well as the opening of Russian schools everywhere, doing everything possible to destroy Polish propaganda and any function of their administrative system, and cancelling all their external signs. We must not allow the Polish people any position in the administrative system." From *Pamietniki Michala Mikolajewicza Murawiewa Wieszatiela* (Biblioteka Orla Bialego: Wlochy, 1945), pp. 85, 105, 127.

21. Cf. O. Filek, *Przedmowa*, in Czeslaw Gil, *Ojciec Rafal Kalinowski* (Krakow, 1979), p. 6 (henceforth cited as OR, with the page number).

22. One of the insurrectionists testified: "The Russians themselves called him a Polish saint. And it was this reputation that saved Kalinowski from the gallows. Muraviev wanted to hang him at all cost, but one of his generals pointed out that the Poles and even many Russians venerated him as a saint; and consequently, if he were hanged, he would be venerated as a martyr. Muraviev feared this." W. Nowakowski, *Wilia w Usolu na Syberii 1865 roku* (Krakow, 1894), p. 5.

23. M 90–94.

24. Ibid., 96.

25. This is the way Ilse Leitenberger entitled her biography of Father Raphael in German (*Ein Engel für Tobias*, [Herder, 1983]), gathering up in an exceptional way the most characteristic and fundamental qualities of Father Kalinowski's life. As the angel was for Tobias in the Old Testament, so this new Raphael (as he would later be known in Carmel) became for many a friend and companion on the journey.

26. L 58.

27. Cf. L 58.

28. L 73.

29. It is clear that he wanted to join the Capuchins, because in January 1864 he wrote a letter to Mrs. Luisa Mlocka (with whom he maintained ties of spiritual friendship until his death), explaining to her: "There are requirements and necessary conditions for entering the novitiate.... Please obtain for me the address of the provincial of this Order" (L 40). His desires ended in failure because the Czarist government had closed the monastery.

30. L 86.

31. "The plight of our exiled youth is sad," he himself wrote in a letter. "Forced idleness is the worst thing, and brings about every kind of evil. But there's no remedy" (L 58). However, he himself did find a remedy by

gathering these young people around him, as circumstances permitted, as he began to teach them lessons in collaboration with Father Szwernicki. His greatness of spirit is demonstrated in these words, written to a friend who also wished to dedicate himself to teaching. "The lessons here are very much sought after, so you can easily find a lot of work. I am, however, against your teaching, even if I consider you a good teacher. Until you open youself to the light of Christ, I consider you unprepared for the formation of youth…because you are incapable of understanding the needs of the human soul. I'm writing to you frankly, because I know that you understand how to distinguish sincere friendship from superficiality. You know, my dear friend, how I would like to win you over, for yourself, for others, and for God. Today you don't know how to master yourself.… I'm not arguing about the well-deserved temporal fruits of your labors; but I see that the final goal of life is unclear to you" (L 281).

32. L 274.

33. L 288; cf. 293.

34. Ibid.

35. M 138; L 286, 293, 294.

36. "Gucio [the Polish diminutive for Augustus] is very sick," wrote Joseph in his *Memoirs*. "He has symptoms of pneumonia. The doctors ordered him to leave Paris as soon as possible and go to nearby Mentone, a health resort. From that day onward, he moved from one health resort to another: Mentone, Eaux-Bonnes in the Pyranees, Davos in Switzerland and even Trouville" (pp. 147–148). From other sources we know the pilgrimage of Kalinowski and the prince took him to such places as Avignon, Dijon, Poitiers, Bordeaux, and Lourdes in France; Genoa, Milan, and Venice in Italy; and Berlin in Germany. The two also traveled to Monaco, Gniezno, and Poznan. See Czeslaw Gil, *Ojciec Rafal Kalinowski 1835–1907* (Krakow, 1984), pp. 152–162. Hereafter cited as ORK, with page numbers.

37. L 318, 377; M 141, 146–147.

38. Cf. L 293, 350, 378, 408.

39. Cf. L 354.

40. Recently published by B. Burdziej in *Przeglad Powszechny* (1988, no. 2): 169–171.

41. Ibid.

42. Cf. Czeslaw Gil, "Sette lettere sconosciute del b. Raffaele Kalinowski," *Teresianum* 40 (1989): 189.

43. L 390.

44. M 113–114.

45. Better known under the religious name of Sister Mary Saveria of Jesus (1833–1928).

46. The Discalced Carmelites came to Poland in 1605 and founded their first monastery at Cracow. This was the seed of the monasteries later founded in Poland and Lithuania. The Polish province of the Order was established in 1617. In the eighteenth century there were seventeen

monasteries of friars and eight of the nuns, divided into two independent provinces: the Polish province of the Holy Spirit, and the Lithuanian province of Saint Casimir. By the middle of the eighteenth century the Polish province had 324 religious and seven monasteries of Carmelite nuns; the Lithuanian Province, on the other hand, had 153 religious and one convent of nuns. Due to suppressions that occurred after the partition of Poland, by the second half of the eighteenth century there remained only one monastery of friars (that of Czerna near Cracow) and only one convent of nuns (at Cracow), who were then juridically incorporated into the semi-province of Austria-Hungary. See J.B. Wanat, *Zakon Karmelitow Bosych w Polsce 1605–1975* (Krakow, 1979), pp. 55–70.

47. In the *Chronicles* of the monastery we find a little notice about the spiritual intentions for which the community was to pray. The first thing we read is: "Our Order in Poland, Mr. Kalinowski" (cf. ORK 164, note 92).

48. L 378. The citation of Teresa's "Bookmark" is completed and the translation taken from *The Collected Works of St. Teresa of Avila*, trans. Kieran Kavanaugh and Otilio Rodriguez (Washington, DC: ICS Publications, 1985), p. 386.

49. L 387.

50. L 390. One week later he wrote: "It has been thirteen years since it pleased the Lord to awaken in me a constant desire to dedicate myself to him in the religious life. External obstacles prevented me, but now the Lord has eliminated them. But one other difficulty has appeared: the choice of a suitable Order. I have struggled with this problem during the last two years. Today I consider this call to Carmel as inspired by God." (L 386)

51. Even the young prince Augustus some years later received a call to enter religious life and was clothed with the Salesian habit by Saint John Bosco at Turin. After Augustus's death in 1893, the process for his beatification was initiated. In November 1978, John Paul II signed the decree of the heroicity of his virtues.

52. Cf. *Chronicles* of the monastery of Czerna of the Discalced Carmelite friars, vol. II, p. 124, where we read this note: "Reverend Father Raphael often said: If God called me to Carmel, I owe it to them; I owe everything to our nuns." The same Father Raphael confesses in a letter addressed to the Polish nuns: "It seems to me that I alone know you better than anyone, and I understand better, with the heart of a brother, the needs of every one of you" (L 1230).

53. Cfr. Valentine Macca, "Raphael of Saint Joseph," in *Saints of Carmel*, edited by Louis Saggi (Carmelite Institute: Rome, 1972), pp. 256. Father Raphael's activities regarding the Discalced Carmelite nuns are carefully analyzed by Czeslaw Gil, ORK 234–236.

54. Cf. C 24 and 25; *Perfectae Caritatis*, 5. In the second part of our study we will take up this theme in greater detail.

55. Even to this day, most of the religious in the renewed Polish Discalced Carmelite provinces are the alumni of the little college, which

had both glorious and sad moments in its history. During the Stalinist era, for example, most of the buildings were confiscated and converted into municipal hospitals. Today, in the wake of "perestroika," the little college, now called a minor seminary, enjoys the rights of a state school and is recognized by civil authorities.

56. Cf. ORK 336–339.

57. *Klasztory Karmelitanek Bosych w Polsce, na Litwie i Rusi...,* vols. I–IV, (Krakow, 1900–1904).

58. Od Sw. Teresy H. [Czeslaw Gil], "Wklad Slugi Bozego O. Rafala Kalinowskiego w odnowe Prowincji Polskiej," in *Karmel* (1981, no. 4), p. 75; see M. Machejek, *Karmel Terezjanski w Polsce* (Rome, 1966), p. 12.

59. Best remembered is his biography of Mother Teresa of Jesus Marchocka (1603–1652), foundress of the convents of Warsaw and Leopoli, called the "Polish Teresa of Jesus." It was published in French as *Vie et vertus héroiques de la Mère Thérèse de Jésus (Marchocka)* (Lille-Paris-Bruges, 1906). Father Raphael worked diligently to have her cause of beatification introduced. In the elaboration published in *Notificationes e Curia Episcopali Dioecesis Cracowiensis* (1882, no. 9), pp. 10–15, for the third centenary of the death of Saint Teresa, he presented her life and doctrine and the situation of the Teresian Carmel in Poland. Again, in a study he presented for a collection commemorating for the fiftieth anniversary of the dogma of the Immaculate Conception (*Ksiega Pamiatkowa Marianska* [Lwow-Warszawa 1905], vol I, part II, pp. 403–427), he describes devotion to Our Lady of Mount Carmel in the Polish Carmel, in convents still existing and in those long supressed. For the beatification of the Carmelite martyrs of Sumatra, Denis and Redemptus, when Father Raphael published the 47-page booklet *Blogoslawieni O. Dionizy od Narodzenia i Br Redemptus od Krzyza* (Krakow, 1900), he added a footnote on the martyrdom of eighteenth-century Polish Carmelites at Wisnicz and at Przemysl. He also tried to reprint a book on the Marian shrine of the Discalced Carmelites at Berdicev in the Ukraine (cf. L 1114, ORK 322); he wanted to write a little book on the Shrine of the Madonna of Mercy at Vilna (cf. ORK, 317–318; L 752, 837, 839, 845, 848); and he collaborated with Father Jean-Baptiste Bouchaud who collected material on devotion to Saint Joseph in the suppressed monasteries (cf. L 1631 as well as L 6; "Sette lettere sconosciute," p. 206), etc.

60. He prepared a Polish edition of St. John of the Cross's *Sayings of Light and Love* (cf. ORK 328–329); a book on the sixteen Carmelite nuns martyred at Compiègne entitled *Szesnascie Karmelitanek Bosych meczenniczek straconych w czasie wielkiej Rewolucji Francuskiej 17 VIII 1794* (Krakow, 1906); a biography of Father Hermann Cohen, the famous Jewish musician and convert who became a Discalced Carmelite, entitled *Zycie O. Hermana, w Zakonie Augustyna Maryi od Najsw. Sakramentu, karmelity* (Krakow, 1898); and a tribute to the Madonna of Carmel, *O koronce Szkaplerznej Matki Boskiej z Gory Karmelu* (cf. ORK 328).

61. The inhabitants of Silesia, faithful to the traditions of their ancestors, still come to Czerna today, and not only for the Madonna, but also to venerate the mortal remains of the one who propagated her devotion and today shares her glory. Recall that in 1966 Karol Wojtyla, Archbishop of Cracow, returned to the Shrine at Czerna and said: "I rejoice greatly that in this Monastery of Czerna, near the tomb of Father Raphael, the nearby diocece of Katowice is praying with us. It is not by accident nor is it an isolated fact, because for years our brothers and sisters of Silesia have been coming to Czerna: the faithful, priests, and even bishops. I rejoice that the bishop of Katowice is with us, with a representation of his faithful." Our translation of this exhortation into Italian can be found in its entirety in *Rivista di Vita Spirituale* 37 (1983) 308–313.

62. Cf. ORK 314–315; L 1224.

63. The Opening Prayer of the Mass in honor of Saint Raphael stresses his "extraordinary and burning charity for the unity of the church." All these aspects will be dealt with at greater length in the second part of this study.

64. L 1103.

65. Cf. the Prayer after Communion for his feast on November 15, in the Carmelite Missal.

NOTES TO PART II

1. Cf. Romuald Od Sw. Eliasza, *Wspomnienie posmiertne o sp. O.Rafale Kalinowskim, karmelicie bosym, usczestniku powstania z roku 1863, dlugoletnim Sybiraku i wygynancu* (Krakow, 1908), 28; J.Gieysztor, *Pamietniki z lat 1857-1865* (Vilnius, 1921), 46-47 and 143.

2. Some reminiscences of those who knew Kalinowski have been published by Cz. Gil in *Ojciec Rafal Kalinowski* [hereafter OR] (Krakow, 1979), 77-102.

3. L 60.

4. Nowakowski, ibid.

5. Cf. V. Macca, "Profeta fortemente impegnato in un'adorazione di supplica," in *L'Osservatore Romano* (November 8, 1980), 5.

6. L 952.

7. Cf. Vatican Council II, *Apostolicam actuositatem;* John Paul II, *Christifideles laici.*

8. This work was carried out above all by means of his letter writing in prison, in exile, and in Paris; the letters are full of advice and encouragement regarding the Christian life. Joseph's great faith, to which he invites his parents and brothers, is truly remarkable, and he asks them to pray for his companions in misfortune in Siberia who often became indifferent; he asks them to send books and religious objects to use in his apostolate, etc. He suggests the road to priesthood or religious consecration to his brothers

Alexander and George (the latter in fact became a priest); Victor and Mary are invited to participate often in the sacraments, etc. A detailed analysis of this work of Joseph's is found in W. Slomka, "Bl. Rafal Kalinowski jako wychowawca i przewodnik w zyciu duchowo-religijnym," in AA.VV., *W bliskosci Boga* (Krakow, 1986), 225-231.

9. Cf. L 58.

10. Cf. L 92.

11. Cf. L 99; ORK, 99-101.

12. M 116ff.; ORK 111-112.

13. "I will have him under my care like a son," Joseph wrote to a friend Louise Mlocka (L 111); and to his mother he adds: "I undertook this step after long reflection, determined to be a father to him, offering him as much as I myself received in my father's house" (L 112; cf. L 113).

14. Cf. L 114, 116, 120, 122, 127, 128.

15. He moved to Tobolsk to the house of some relatives (cf. L 129, 131 and 136).

16. Cf. L 146, 148, 149.

17. Cf. L 181.

18. Cf. L 249, 253, 260.

19. Cf. L 318, 344, 346, 360, 377, 391, 420.

20. Cf. L 391, 392, 399.

21. Cf. M 147.

22. L 62.

23. L 95.

24. L 102; cf. L 58 and 62.

25. L 73.

26. "I had very sincere and cordial ties of friendship with the late Father Raphael, Joseph Kalinowski. Every time I went from Kultuk to Irkutsk I would see him, and he would come to our house too when we were living in Kultuk. He drew several anatomical details for my work on the seals of Lake Baikal.... When Joseph was already a religious and came to Leopoli, we would always see each other, and on different occasions we would speak with Father Nowakowski, a Capuchin, on the fight against alcoholism.... This was our relationship as friends, which we maintained throughout our life despite our diverse opinions on human existence and the world. If we were to consider someone a saint, Father Raphael would be in the first rank. He had all the qualities of an angel and not a single human imperfection. His angelic forbearance, his love for humanity, his consideration and respect for the ideas of others, etc., made him an exceptional man. People like this are not easy to find in our days" (testimonial related in OR, 83-84).

27. Cf. ORK 117-118, 208, 302.

28. Cf. *Apostolicam actuositatem*, 16.

29. The subject is treated at length by M. Machejek, "Bl. Rafal Kalinowski wzorem spowiednika dusz," in *Duszpasterz Polski Zagranica* 35 (1984) 376-383; OR 62-70; ORK 294-302 and 309-315.

30. L 58. Father Feliciano Antoniewicz (died 1869), Kalinowski's confessor, was a professor in the seminary of Vilnius.

31. L 67.

32. Cf. 72, 73, 75, 77, 81, 86, 87.

33. Cf. L 122 and 181.

34. We have recalled above Joseph's collaboration with Father Szwernicki (cf. L 92, 99, 108, etc.).

35. Cf. L 259.

36. Cf. *Cracovien: Beatificationis et canonizationis S. D. Raphaëlis a S. Joseph.... Summarium super virtutibus,* 104, 962.

37. Ibid., 962.

38. Cf. M Machejek, op. cit., 378-379.

39. Testimonial contained in ORK 309-310. Numerous other testimonials are found in *Summarium super virtutibus,* op. cit., 80,104, 327.

40. C 29. [See the text on pages 42–46 of this volume.—Trans.]

41. "To use the noun *confession* constitutes an impoverishment of the global meaning of the Sacrament of Penance" (C 29, 5).

42. C 29, 4.

43. Cf. L 1288.

44. C 29, 6.

45. C 29, 7.

46. C 29, 10.

47. To a penitent, a sister who continually asked for a general confession [*Generalbeichte*], the Saint answered: "One would have thought that your Reverence was a native of Silesia: *Generalbeicht, Generalbeicht,* limitless and without end. To deplore our past sins, to thank Our Lord for having forgiven them, to try by our present life to make amends for former days and, if here or there we fall into some infidelity, to humble ourselves and ask for the grace to avoid these as much as possible in the future" (L 1031; cf. L 1486).

48. C 29, 4.

49. C 32, 1; 9, 5; 22, 3; 39, 3. Cf. Col 1:24.

50. C 1, 43.

51. Cf. L 632; C 2, 5.

52. This doctrine, intuited by Kalinowski, has been confirmed in our times by Paul VI's *Solemn Profession of Faith:* "We believe that the Most Holy Mother of God ... continues in heaven her maternal role to the members of the church, cooperating in the birth and development of divine life in the souls of the redeemed" (AAS 60 (1968) 438-439; cf. *Redemptoris Mater,* n. 47).

53. *De cultura Ordinis: Sinopsis animadversionum ad documentum laboris* (Rome: Casa Generalizia OCD, 1985), 43.

54. "Czesc Matki Bozej w Karmelu Polskim," in *Ksiega Pamiatkowa Marianska* (Lwov-Warsaw, 1905), vol. 1, part 2, 426.

55. Ibid., 426-427.

56. Cf. M 6-7 (Bishop Siemaszko's schism and the occupation of Uniate churches by the Orthodox in Vilnius); pp. 53 and 129 (the low cultural level of the Orthodox clergy); p. 57 (the destruction of Uniate churches and monuments in Brest); p. 73 (the presence of Old Catholics in Kowno); p. 125 (Protestants in Perm); pp. 129-130 (Orthodox occupation of Catholic churches in Lithuania).

57. L 81.

58. M 85.

59. Ibid., 114.

60. We have now seen evidence of what he thought while still in Siberia: "precisely the Carmelite Order should make the Eastern schismatics return to the breast of the Church of Rome" (M 113).

61. L 949.

62. Cf. L 897.

63. Cf. L 887, 925, 927, 930, 938, 952, 968 and 1081. Father Raphael was helped in this work by Father J. Wasilewski, SJ, mentioned earlier, and by two penitents, Fanny Jelinek and Teresa Moruzi.

64. L 952.

65. Father Raphael's intuition finds a strong echo in the conciliar document on ecumenism (*Unitatis redintegratio*) that, in number 15, treats of the elements that unite us with the Eastern Churches, emphasizing, among other things, devotion to the Blessed Virgin Mary. So does *Lumen Gentium*, no. 69. John Paul II also brings up the same aspects in *Redemptoris Mater*, 33.

66. Cf. L 1012, 1057, 1106, 1211, 1667, 1712; M 7; Czesc, op.cit., 407, 411, 422-423.

67. Cf. C 35, 4.

68. Ibid., 32, 2.

69. Cf. ORK 295.

70. Cf. M 137; ORK 295.

71. Cf. Ibid.

72. *Perfectae caritatis*, 5.

73. C 24, 10.13; 25, 5. Elsewhere he will say the same thing, referring to the nuns and sisters.

74. C 24, 6.

75. H. Gil writes on our Saint's theology of the religious life in "Zakonnica jest tylko chrzescijanka: Bl. Rafal Kalinowski o powolaniu Karmelitanki," in *Karmel* (Krakow) 7 (1986) no. 3 (20) 17-30.

76. *Cracovien: Beatificationis et canonizationis S. D. Raphaëelis a S. Joseph...: Relatio et vota Congressus peculiaris super virtutibus*, 7.

77. Regarding this matter, see our essays: "Rola Matki Bozej w zyciu bl. Rafala Kalinowskiego," in *Homo Dei* 53 (1984): 54-75; ""Maria sempre e in tutto'—dice il beato Raffaele Kalinowski," in *Fiamma Teresiana* 26 (1985): 84-89.

78. Cf. *Lumen Gentium*, chap. 8: "De Beata Maria Vergine Deipara in mysterio *Christi* et *Ecclesiae.*"

79. In his *Memoirs* (p. 55) Kalinowski confesses that after finishing his studies, when he was in the solitude of the countryside to plan of the Kursk-Konotop railroad, a sense of faith in the intercession of the Madonna reawakened in him thanks to a devotional book that happened into his hands: "With her help I have been able to build up my interior life. I recognized the value of familiar religious principles and, finally, I turned toward them." Then, on the feast of the Assumption in 1863, he went to confession, thereby beginning by means of the sacramental ministry a new life that kept developing (cf. L 11; ORK 292).

80. Such were his thoughts in Siberia when he learned that there was an Order (Carmel) that was born in the East and moved to the West: "Precisely this Order should make the Eastern schismatics return to the breast of the Church of Rome" (M 113).

81. C 8, 6, 9.

82. In a conference to his religious confreres, given on the vigil of the solemnity of Our Lady of Mt. Carmel, he literally affirmed: "We are her work and she does not cease calling us to be her ministers, to take care of her affairs" (C 7, 2).

83. C 8. The Saint evidently never used the expression "the church, universal sacrament of salvation" (which we owe to *Lumen Gentium*, 9); however, he lives out this reality: cf. Cz. Gil, "Duchowosc bl. Rafala Kalinowskiego," in AA.VV., *W bliskosci*, op.cit., 216-220 and 223.

84. For Kalinowski, growth in intimacy with the Virgin Mary was the measure of progress on the way of perfection, a visible sign of the action of the Holy Spirit (cf. L 632; C 2, 5). For this reason he never tired of emphasizing how necessary it is to put oneself in the hands of the Mother of Christ and by means of her to obtain all the necessary graces for the interior life. He based this on the common faith of the church—or, rather, he was a typical representative of the mediationist currents of the last century by which the finding of Christ was accompanied by, if not actually a consequence of, the finding of his Mother (cf. R. Aubert, "La Chiesa cattolica dalla crisi del 1848 alla prima guerra mondiale," in AA.VV., *Nuova Storia della Chiesa* (Turin, 1977),vol. 5/1, 159-160, which venerates Mary as Mediatrix of grace and Help of Christians (cf. *Lumen Gentium*, 61-62; *Redemptoris Mater*, 38ff.). To her he recommended all his penitents, to her he sent them, convinced that she would be a support and refuge for them and that in her they would find not only the answer to their problems, but also and above all help for continual spiritual growth (cf. L 638, 639, 1448, 1449, 1452, 1482, 1686; C 7, 9). The Virgin, according to Father Raphael, participates in a very special way in the process of the purification of souls, until nothing remains in them of the "old man," but the image of the "New Man," Jesus Christ, is fashioned in them (cf. L 1504).

85. Cf. L 80, 432, 501, 519, 887, 925, 927, 930, 938, 952, 968, 1026; C 7, 8.

86. C 25, 7.

NOTES TO PART III

1. In 1869, reflecting in exile on the fate of those souls who die without membership in the church, Kalinowski wrote in his *Siberian Journal:* "The Catholic Church, convinced that outside herself there is no salvation, invites all persons to belong to it, and prays for their conversion so that they might enter, already on this earth, upon the way of salvation.... But if a person dies outside the body of the Catholic Church only through *ignorantia invincibilis* [invincible ignorance], that person, belonging *ipso facto* to the soul of the church, participates in the graces God confers on the faithful through the prayers of the church" (C 1, 2). These words echo the teachings of the Magisterium: *Lumen Gentium,* 14-17; *Unitatis Redintegratio,* 5; *Ad Gentes,* 7.

2. From PN 17, "Living on Love," in Thérèse of Lisieux, Poetry, trans. Donald Kinney (Washington, DC: ICS Publications, 1995). This poem is also known by the title, "To Live by Love."

3. Solomon, to whom the Song of Songs (or Canticle of Canticles) was traditionally attributed.

4. Raphael Kalinowski is alluding to the pastoral visit he is conducting as Vicar Provincial for the nuns.

The Institute of Carmelite Studies promotes research and publication in the field of Carmelite spirituality. Its members are Discalced Carmelites, part of a Roman Catholic community—friars, nuns, and laity—who are heirs to the teaching and way of life of Teresa of Jesus and John of the Cross, men and women dedicated to contemplation and to ministry in the church and the world. Information concerning their way of life is available through local diocesan Vocation Offices, or from the Vocation Director's Office, 1525 Carmel Road, Hubertus, WI, 53033.